COLLINS HANDGUIDE TO THE

BIRDS

OF NEW ZEALAND

Written and painted by
Chlöe Talbot Kelly

Designed by **Herman Heinzel**

Collins
AUCKLAND   SYDNEY   LONDON

Acknowledgments

The author wishes to thank the following for their help in the preparation of this book:

Derek Goodwin and the staff of the Bird Room at the British Museum (Natural History), Tring, England; the staff of the National Museum, Wellington, New Zealand; Mr F. C. Kinsky, Nancy M. Adams, Elizabeth Loosmore, Dorothy Talbot Kelly and Michael and Carole Hudson of Hawke's Bay, New Zealand.

Jacket illustrations: *(Front)* Fantail, *Rhipidura fuliginosa;* *(Back)* North Island Saddleback, *Philesturnus carunculatus rufusater.*
Title page illustration: Rifleman, *Acanthisitta chloris.*

William Collins Publishers Ltd
P.O. Box 1, Auckland

First published 1982
© Chlöe Talbot Kelly
ISBN 0 00 216533 3

Colour reproduction by Adroit Photo Litho Ltd, Birmingham
Filmsetting by Jacobson Typesetters Ltd, Auckland
Printed in Hong Kong

Contents

The birds shown in this contents list are not to a common scale. All are adult males in breeding plumage. If females differ they, together with juveniles and non-breeding birds, will be found on the pages indicated below. Backgrounds indicate the kind of habitat in which these birds may be found.

Herons, Spoonbills, Ibis and Bittern 46-49

Geese and Swans 50-51

Ducks and Grebes 52-57

Falcons and Harriers 58-59

Guineafowl and Quail 62-63

Pheasants and Partridges 60-61

Turkey and Peafowl 64-65

Rails, Crakes and Coots 66-69

Waders 70-79

Introduction

This book is a guide for those who enjoy the countryside. It is intended to help them to identify the birds they see and to tell them how to find rarer species. It is very easy to get lost in the New Zealand bush. Human speech seems to be mere lisping when heard against the sibilance of the cicadas and bird song is scarce. If no birds seem to be about try this ruse with a small glass bottle and a piece of cork. Moisten the cork and rub it up and down against the bottle. The noise produced will sound like a small bird announcing a good source of food. This will attract other small birds, which may be very tame.

Seventy million years ago a land bridge still connected New Zealand to the mainland. Over this the ancestors of the Kiwis and the Moas crossed, but only two mammals, both bats, managed to establish themselves. After the separation of New Zealand from the land mass the ancestors of Wekas, Kakapos and Takahes flew over from Australia on the prevailing west-east winds. There were no carnivorous predators to attack them and these birds gradually lost the power of flight. Later came the unique native Wrens, Wattlebirds and Thrushes, and even today colonisation still occurs. Some species long-resident in New Zealand show no appreciable difference from their Australian cousins while others have developed into distinct sub-species.

When the Polynesians arrived with their dogs over a thousand years ago they found 24 different species of Moas alone. The flightless birds were easy prey and a ready source of protein. A few of the larger species survived until the advent of the Europeans in the seventeenth century but, by the nineteenth century, the last species was extinct, although rumours of sightings still occur.

Extinction of a species is a continuing process brought about by climatic changes, destruction of habitat, predation and competition from other species. Although the Polynesian settlers burnt off much of the vegetation, the greatest impact on the countryside has been made in the last 170 years and many native species now survive only in the outlying islands.

Almost 70 per cent of the original native bush has been totally destroyed and a large part of the remainder has been profoundly affected by the introduction of Red Deer. Native birds have been further reduced since the introduction of the weasel family. Land has been turned over to arable farming, to sheep and cattle; exotic trees and shrubs have been planted and many alien species of birds have been introduced.

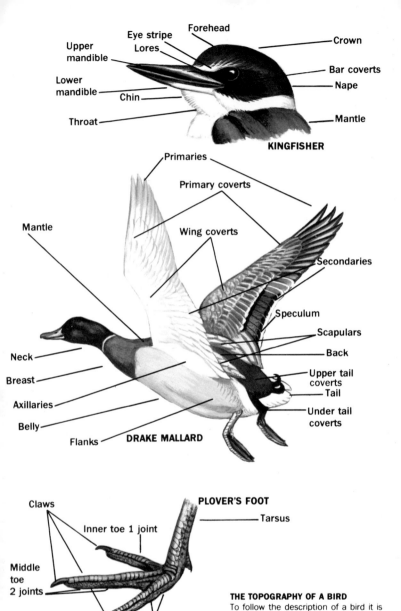

KINGFISHER

Forehead
Eye stripe
Crown
Upper mandible
Lores
Bar coverts
Lower mandible
Nape
Chin
Throat
Mantle

DRAKE MALLARD

Primaries
Primary coverts
Wing coverts
Mantle
Secondaries
Speculum
Scapulars
Back
Neck
Breast
Upper tail coverts
Tail
Axillaries
Under tail coverts
Belly
Flanks

PLOVER'S FOOT

Claws
Inner toe 1 joint
Tarsus
Middle toe 2 joints
Outer toe 3 joints

THE TOPOGRAPHY OF A BIRD
To follow the description of a bird it is necessary to understand the terms used to describe feather groups and physical features.

Bird recognition

There are many things to look for in seeking to identify a particular bird. Take note of the shape and length of its bill, for birds have evolved their bills into specialised feeding tools. Waders' bills are long and thin, the length varying with the depth of mud and sand in which their invertebrate prey may be found. The finches have powerful seed-crushing bills. Notice how the legs and feet of birds differ. Duck, geese and many seabirds have webbed feet, while rails and waders have long slim toes and falcons the powerful claws and toes of a bird that uses them for killing. Parrots and cuckoos are zygodactylus: they have two toes pointing forwards and two pointing backwards, a useful sort of foot for holdings things. To eat their food parrots often hold it in one foot. Birds also 'wear' their wings and tails differently from each other. Some hold closed wings high enough to show both upper and lower tail coverts, while others cock their tails and drop their wings, as do the introduced blackbirds and thrushes and the native Tomtits. No species of bird is quite like another and their individual characteristic ways of walking, hopping, perching or flying enable the experienced watcher to identify them by their shapes alone.

Birdsong

Birdsong is in part innate, in part learned, and calls associated with territory are generally produced by males alone. In some species both sexes sing, often in duet. For instance, a pair of Saddlebacks will chatter loudly and constantly together, or the female will chatter while the male sings the species song, which has an added dialect learned, not from the parent bird, but from the song of a near neighbour. Saddlebacks will sing from the centre of their territories, deep in the bush. Other species, the Yellowhammers among them, often have favourite branches or prominent posts on the borders of their territories from which they sing in full view. Birds that nest in the open, and often on the ground, may sing and call on the wing. The waders and especially skylarks, are such species. Although males generally do most of the singing it is the females who do so if they initiate the

A Saddleback calling

Skuas make loud calls near their nesting sites

courtship, as do the Phalaropes. Once a male has attracted his mate, his solos, or their duets, strengthen the pair-bond and, in dense bush, keep the pair in touch as well as warning off other males of the same species. There seems to be no biological explanation for the many elaborations and variations in some birds' songs. They may sing to use up surplus energy or for sheer *joie de vivre*.

Territory

Territory is the area defended by one bird, or a pair, against other members of the same species, particularly, in the breeding season, against other males. The territory owner patrols his boundaries, sings from prominent positions and may drive off all intruders by aggressive displays. A territory may vary in size from a very large area to little more than the spot on which the nest is built. Birds that nest in hollows in cliffs or trees, where there may be few possible sites, hold well-spaced-out territories. The colonial nesters which congregate together on the ground in thousands, as do Gannets at Cape Kidnappers, defend areas no larger than the limits of their bills' reach as they sit on the nest. Generally a lot of squabbling results. Spacing probably avoids interference with mating, reserves enough food for the pair and its family and may avoid excessive loss from predators. Birds may become so attached to a site that they will return to it year after year, even after man has radically altered it, for instance by building an airport on the spot. Site attachment leads to a detailed topographical knowledge of the area and its food resources which has considerable survival value. A defended territory warns those birds without one not to waste time in that particular area, an owner generally wins, and many potential fights are warded off by threats alone. Some species defend their territories for one breeding season only; others are held by birds who live and breed in them year after year, driving away all others of their species including their own fully-fledged young.

Courtship

Most birds have one breeding season each year, the length of which depends upon internal stimuli. It is not known whether there is any external influence, though the relative abundance of food will affect the number of broods reared. The majority of birds pair for at least one breeding season, others remain paired for life. The male usually initiates courtship with song, song-flights or special displays. Intruding males are driven off and, once attracted, the female's submissive behaviour leads to her recognition and the pair is formed. They continue to display throughout breeding. In geese, for instance, there is a mutual greeting ceremony at every change-over or arrival at the nest. This helps to cement the bond between the pair. Some birds bring 'presents' in their displays; a heron will bring a stick or twig for its mate to add to the nest, and starlings push flowers for their mates into the nesting holes.

Nests and Eggs

Birds breed in a great variety of places, building nests in holes in trees, cliffs, logs or buildings, holes excavated in banks by the birds themselves, or utilising the empty nests of other species. The nest may be as elaborate as that of the Silvereye, made of tough grasses, horsehair, cobwebs and moss suspended from a twig, preferably from a fork, or as simple as the slight scoop in the sand in which the New Zealand Dotterel lays her eggs.

Some birds nest alone in the centre of their territories, some nest on the ground in the open, either alone or in large colonies, sometimes nesting very close to each other, sometimes well spaced out. Some species return to the same nest or nesting site year after year, while others which rear several broods in a season may build a new nest for each family. (This may be to avoid parasitic infestation.) Both sexes usually contribute to building

Heron courtship

Silvereye's nest

New Zealand Dotterel's scoop nest

the nest. One may build while the other fetches nesting material, both may build and fetch, or one may undertake both tasks alone.

Eggs vary enormously, but those of any one species are always alike. Their size varies from the very large eggs that the Kiwis lay to the small ones of the songbirds. In texture they may be matt or powdery, or oily or greasy, as are those of some seabirds, ducks and geese. They may be pure white, cream or various colours, with or without spots or blotches. Some are almost round, others have various oval or elliptical shapes and some are pointed or conical. The latter, if laid in threes or fours, are arranged with their points to the centre of the group, so giving the parent a smaller area to brood, or if they are the single eggs of cliff-nesting birds their conical shape prevents them rolling off the ledge. The number of broods in any one season, and the successful rearing of the maximum number of chicks, depends upon climate, food supplies and predators.

Cuckoos lay their eggs in the nests of other species and the single, relatively vast, young is reared at the expense of every nestling of the host species. As soon as it hatches the baby cuckoo rolls every other egg in the nest up and out of it.

Some birds develop on their breasts a bare patch of skin, richly supplied with blood vessels for extra heat. This is called a brood patch. Ducks and geese, however, make their own. They pluck feathers and down from their breasts and use them as nest lining.

Food

There is hardly a creature that crawls or flies, a plant that grows or a small animal living in mud, sand, rotting bark, shallow water or in the upper layers of deep water that is not the food of one bird or another. Birds may themselves be prey and, dead, may become the food of those amongst them that are carrion eaters and scavengers.

Closely related species manage to live in the same habitat without competing with each other because each has evolved into a specialised feeder, with the tools required to gain its food. Bills are probes, hammers and crushing instruments or are equipped with fine filters to sieve minute food particles from water. Birds that hawk insects on the wing have bills which look very small when closed but which open into vast gapes, generally having stiff bristles on either side to help prevent the insects from escaping. Feet, as well as bills, are used to hold down, lift up, dig and scratch for food and for killing. Owls and other birds of prey have powerful talons for this purpose. Some birds are completely vegetarian, the New Zealand Pigeon for instance, which eats the leaves of many shrubs and trees as well as their fruits. Skuas chase and harry other seabirds until they drop or disgorge the fish that they have caught and both skuas and gulls will kill and eat the young of any bird not their own that is not too large or too well guarded.

Generally a bird hunts for food for itself alone (or for its family in the breeding season) but some hunt together: cormorants fish in long lines over shoals and pelicans herd fish cooperatively. Birds also follow sheep and cattle and feed on the insects put up by their grazing, while others ride their backs to search for and remove ticks.

If the watcher is very lucky he may come across a bird army. If an insect species builds up massive numbers or the ground smokes with the nuptial flight of ants it will attract many different species of insectivorous birds. As they congregate to gorge themselves the noise they make may be heard from a long way off.

Habitat

Birds will seek the habitat which enables them to rear successfully the maximum number of young, choosing it as their breeding area, even though they may not live there all the year round. Those that migrate from area to area may be said to have several habitats therefore, and are not sedentary species.

The existence of other species in an area leads to specialisation in food needs and nesting requirements so that competition between species is reduced. Man has radically altered the countryside with his farming methods and destruction of native bush. By so doing he has started a succession of changes with the result that some species of birds have become extinct, have been forced into other habitats or have learned to adapt to the changes. The study of the type of vegetation in an area and some knowledge of breeding requirements, climatic needs and migration patterns help the birdwatcher to know which species he should be looking for and how to find them.

Migration

Migration is the seasonal movement of birds from one area to another. Most species migrate, if only for short distances, so for the purpose of this book all species are assumed to migrate unless referred to as sedentary species (the Dominican Gull is one such). New Zealand attracts many migrants, in particular waders and seabirds. Estuaries are among the best places to watch such birds and many native species are also found there. New Zealand is a country in which the ranges of different species overlap in a fashion which seems unusual to northern hemisphere observers. Parrots, for instance, may be found in the same areas as penguins.

Migration is an alternative to complete adaptation to one area. In the event of natural or man-made disasters the migrant bird has considerable survival advantages. In the past the appearance and disappearance of various birds at regular intervals was put down to hibernation. The discovery of the odd individual when all other members of its kind were gone seemed to confirm this. The hormone changes in the individual bird trigger off the reaction. Most species have definite periods during which migration starts and finishes and most will have left their breeding or wintering grounds at the end of that period. Migration may secure the best food supplies in many areas, provide better nesting conditions and longer daylight hours for food foraging and enable the migratory species to rear more young than the sedentary bird.

The distances travelled on migration differ widely. One species will cross

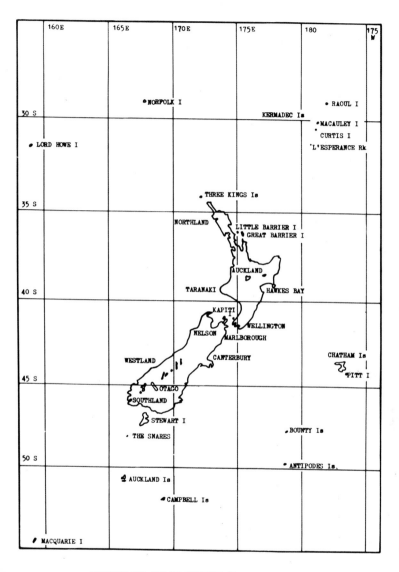

NEW ZEALAND AND ITS OUTLYING ISLANDS

whole oceans and continents while another takes a short flight down from mountain heights to sheltered valleys below. Some seabirds and waders migrate from the temperate zone in the southern hemisphere to the temperate zone in the northern hemisphere and later reverse the process. However, no land bird does this. Sometimes birds move from east to west, and back; from temperate region to tropical, from blustery coastal waters to warmer inland seas. In the tropics migration depends upon wet and dry seasons. Some species breed in the former, others in the latter, each moving elsewhere in the off-seasons.

Some birds migrate during the nights and days, some by day only, others at night only. Shy and secretive species and most small songbirds go by night. When crossing water or flying against strong winds birds fly low but they will fly at considerable altitudes to cross mountain ranges. Bird navigation is a puzzle. Some seabirds have been captured on their nests, transported hundreds or even two or three thousand kilometres away and released in totally unfamiliar surroundings, yet, if they were able to see the sun, or sense it behind thin hazy clouds, they have been able to find their way back again, apparently by the most direct route, in remarkably short time. If thick cloud made this impossible the birds became confused and appeared to be unable to tell in which direction to go. Do they have an internal 'computer' to plot the sun's arc through the sky? Can they see the stars by day as well as by night? Such things are not yet known and how birds find their way is not yet understood, but it is certain that they do use vision and in short journeys local landmarks are of great use.

LITTLE SPOTTED KIWI

KIWI *Apteryx* sp. 35-46 cm The national bird of New Zealand, the Kiwi is a flightless, hairy-looking offshoot of the rattite birds – Moas and Ostriches. There are three species of Kiwi, one with three subspecies: **South Island Brown** *Apteryx australis australis*, **North Island Brown** *A.a.mantelli*, the similar **Stewart Island Brown** *A.a.lawryi*, **Great Spotted** *A.haastii*, and **Little Spotted** *A.oweni*. The Kiwi's long slender bill has nostrils at the end of the upper mandible, the tip of which overhangs that of the lower, and there are tactile bristles around the gape. Its earholes are prominent and easy to see. Its wings are little more than remnants hidden beneath hair-like plumage. Kiwis have powerful legs and toes and long claws. The females are larger than the males. The feathers of the North Island Brown are stiff-tipped and harsh to touch and it is smaller than the South Island race. The two Spotted Kiwis are found in the South Island only.

Kiwis are mainly nocturnal but when released in daylight can see well enough to avoid obstacles as they run. Not strictly forest dwellers, they have adapted well to rough farmland and many are killed on roads. They eat fruit, insects and worms. When hunting worms and insect larvae they will plunge their entire bills into the ground. Early in the morning or evening they may be heard snuffling and puffing out through their nostrils as they forage for food. The bird gets its name from the male's cry; the female makes a hoarse noise. They nest in natural or excavated holes under stones, in stream banks, between tree roots or even on open, flat ground. The female lays 1 or 2 highly-glazed, ivory-white or greenish eggs which are very large and may weigh up to one quarter of the weight of the adult bird. Eggs are usually incubated by the male.

GREAT SPOTTED KIWI

SOUTH ISLAND BROWN KIWI

NORTH ISLAND BROWN KIWI

GENTOO PENGUIN

YELLOW-EYED
PENGUIN

KING PENGUIN

20

KING PENGUIN *Aptenodytes patagonicus* 92 cm King Penguins breed in colonies at Macquarie and spend half their lives at sea feeding on plankton, fish and squid. Both parents incubate the single egg on their feet, under a fold of skin. The yellow of the immatures is paler and the nestlings have brown down. King Penguins squawk and trumpet shrilly.

GENTOO PENGUIN *Pygoscelis papua* 76 cm A sedentary species which breeds at Macquarie, often changing nest sites. The sexes look alike and both incubate their two eggs. Immature birds have mottled throats and poorly defined eye crescents. The nestling's down is similar in pattern to adult plumage: dark above, white below. Gentoos trumpet, bray and hiss.

YELLOW-EYED PENGUIN *Megadyptes antipodes* 76 cm A largely sedentary species which breeds in coastal scrub from Banks Peninsula to Campbell and Auckland Islands. Two eggs are laid. Nestlings wear a uniform, dark, smoky down. The sexes are alike with immatures less strongly marked than adults. They have a great range of calls, some not unlike a Weka's whistle.

BLUE PENGUIN *Eudyptula minor* 40-42 cm Blues are the noisiest of penguins. Their screams, growls, mews and trumpetings may be heard when they come ashore at night. There are five subspecies. The **South Island** race, *E.m.minor*, is darkest blue, the **North Island**, *E.m.iredalei*, has a slimmer bill and the **Cook Strait**, *E.m.variabilis*, is larger and paler with a stouter bill. The **White-flippered**, *E.m.albosignata*, is the more robust. It has a back of pale slate grey and the broad white edges of its flippers sometimes meet in a central patch. It breeds in considerable numbers round the shores of Banks Peninsula. The **Chatham Islands** *E.m.chathamensis*, is as robust as the White-flippered and as dark as the South Island race. Blue Penguins nest in burrows and lay two eggs. Their chicks have sooty-coloured down.

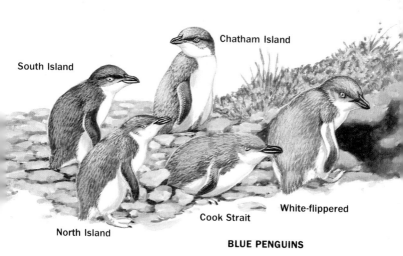

Chatham Island

South Island

White-flippered

Cook Strait

North Island

BLUE PENGUINS

ROCKHOPPER PENGUIN *Eudyptes crestatus* 63 cm Rockhoppers breed in colonies in holes, crevices or open terraces high above the sea, on the rocky coasts of Macquarie, Auckland, Campbell and Antipodes Islands. Immatures have white chins and no crest. Sometimes two downy chicks are reared, dark above and white below. They 'bray' loudly.

ROYAL PENGUIN *Eudyptes schlegeli* 76 cm Royals breed at Macquarie Island, sometimes trekking inland to valleys with streams. Some males are almost indistinguishable from Macaroni Penguins, others have dark throat patches. Few females have completely white faces. Immatures have similar ranges of face patterns. The single chicks are dark above and white below. Royal Penguins 'bray' deeply.

FIORDLAND CRESTED PENGUINS *Eudyptes pachyrhynchus* 71 cm These penguins breed on south and south-western coasts of South and Stewart Islands in caves or under forest roots. Immatures have indistinct head stripes. Two eggs are laid but generally only one chick survives, dark above and dirty white below. Their voice is like a Rockhopper's.

SNARES CRESTED PENGUIN *Eudyptes atratus* 73 cm These penguins breed on Snares Island in dense colonies on bare rock or in clearings near the sea. Immatures have darker bills and few yellow feathers on their heads. Two eggs are laid and two chicks reared. They are smoky brown above, white below. Snares Cresteds bark, whistle, quack and grunt.

ERECT CRESTED PENGUIN *Eudyptes sclateri* 73 cm These penguins breed in colonies at Bounty and Antipodes Islands and, in smaller numbers, at Campbell and Auckland Islands. Immatures have mottled white throats and scarcely-developed crests. They lay two eggs, discarding one. Chicks are sooty black above, white below. Their squawks and yells are resonant.

ROCKHOPPER PENGUIN

light phase

ROYAL PENGUIN

dark phase

SNARES ISLAND CRESTED PENGUIN

ERECT CRESTED PENGUIN

FIORDLAND CRESTED PENGUIN

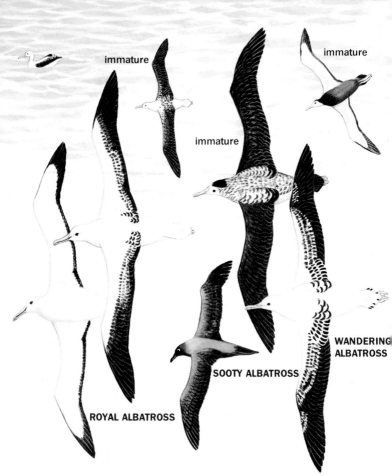

immature

immature

immature

WANDERING ALBATROSS

SOOTY ALBATROSS

ROYAL ALBATROSS

ALBATROSSES Largest of the petrels and amongst the largest of all flying birds, albatrosses have perfected gliding flight. Except in the Pacific they are restricted to the southern hemisphere. Three species breed in New Zealand waters south of latitude 44°. The **Royal Albatross** *Diomedea epomophora epomophora* 75-125 cm nests on Campbell and Auckland Islands, acquiring whiter plumage than a smaller race, *D.e.sandfordi,* which nests on Chatham Island and Otago Peninsula. The **Wandering Albatross**, *D.exulans exulans* 75-125 cm nests on Campbell, Auckland and Antipodes Islands and a larger, snowy-plumaged race, *D.e.chionoptera* nests on Macquarie Island. The **Sooty Albatross** *Phoebetria palpebrata* 70 cm has two forms. The light-mantled nests on Campbell, Auckland, Antipodes and Macquarie Islands but the darker race comes no closer to New Zealand waters than the Australian Bight.

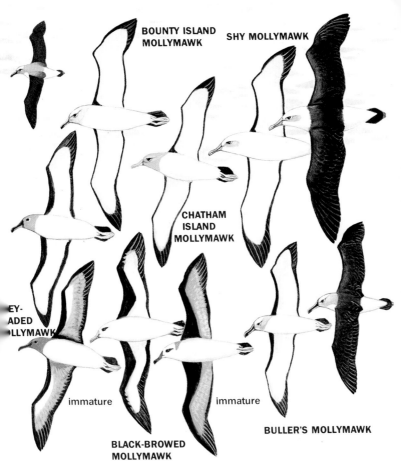

BOUNTY ISLAND MOLLYMAWK

SHY MOLLYMAWK

CHATHAM ISLAND MOLLYMAWK

GREY-HEADED MOLLYMAWK

immature

immature

BLACK-BROWED MOLLYMAWK

BULLER'S MOLLYMAWK

MOLLYMAWKS These smaller albatrosses, usually seen in flight, are recognized by head and bill colours and underwing patterns. The **Black-browed Mollymawk** *Diomedea melanophris* 60 cm has broad black borders to the underwing and the white central area is grey in immatures which have a grey nape to the neck. The **Bounty Island Mollymawk** *D.cauta salvini* 70 cm has a grey back and head, a white crown and a bi-coloured bill (light grey and ivory) with a black tip to the lower mandible. The **Shy Mollymawk** *D.c.cauta* 75 cm has a white head, a black back and no dark on its bill when adult. The **Chatham Island Mollymawk** *D.c.eremita* 70 cm has a bright yellow bill and a darker head than the Shy or Bounty Island. The **Grey-headed Mollymawk** *D.chrysostoma* 63 cm has a still darker head, broad black borders on its underwing leading edge and white feathers around the eye. **Buller's Mollymawk** *D.bulleri* 63 cm has a white forehead and no dark on its bill.

Four families: albatrosses and mollymawks, petrels and shearwaters, storm petrels and finally diving petrels are known as tubenoses from the external tubular nostrils via which surplus salt is removed from their bodies. Their bills are formed of many plates, differing in shape and varying in colour. Albatrosses and mollymawks have relatively small nostrils on the *sides* of their bills. The Giant Petrel has a large tube along the *top* of its bill.

ROYAL ALBATROSS has a bill of pinkish horn with black cutting edges to both mandibles. Immatures have dark wings which become whiter with age, males becoming the whitest.

WANDERING ALBATROSS (below) has a smaller pinkish bill with a yellow tip. Immatures have white faces and underwings with dark brown bodies. In various stages their plumage becomes almost white. Dark-crowned birds are always Wanderings.

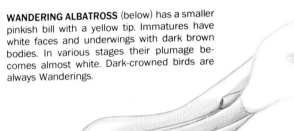

LIGHT-MANTLED SOOTY ALBATROSS is the same size as the mollymawks but differs in shape. The body is light brown and the tail wedged. It has a semi-circle of white feathers round its dark hazel eyes and a very dark chocolate-brown head. The bill is black with, in adult birds, pale blue lines along the lower mandibles.

BLACK-BROWED MOLLY-MAWK has honey-coloured eyes, dark eyebrows and a yellow bill. Immature birds have dark eyes and bills, grey napes and dark grey centres to the underwings which have *broad* black borders.

SHY (WHITE CAPPED) MOLLYMAWK has dark eyes, grey cheeks in females. The bill (immatures darker) is dull yellowish-green, tipped bright yellow. Underwings have *narrow* black borders.

CHATHAM ISLAND MOLLY-MAWK has a pale grey crown, darker cheeks and neck and dark eyes. The bill (immatures darker) is bright yellow with a dark tip to the lower mandible. Underwings have *narrow* black borders.

BOUNTY ISLAND (GREY-BACKED) MOLLY-MAWK has dark eyes, a white crown and grey head and back. The bill (immatures duller) is greeny-grey with darker central area. Underwings have *narrow* black borders.

GREY-HEADED MOLLY-MAWK has a white semi-circle under its dark eyes. The bill (immatures darker) is yellow, tipped with pink with a black central area. Underwings have *broad* black borders.

BULLER'S MOLLYMAWK has dark eyes, white forehead, grey cheeks and nape. The bill is darker in immatures. Underwings have black borders, *broad* on *leading* edges.

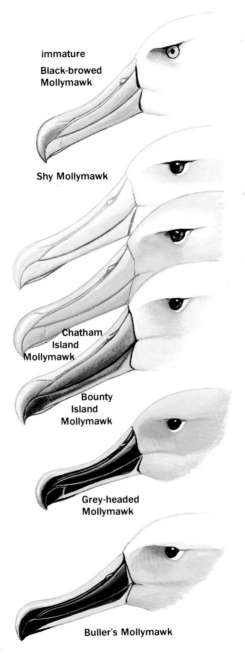

immature
Black-browed Mollymawk

Shy Mollymawk

Chatham Island Mollymawk

Bounty Island Mollymawk

Grey-headed Mollymawk

Buller's Mollymawk

ROYAL ALBATROSS *Diomedea epomophora epomophora* 75-125 cm The sexes are alike though the males are larger and young Royals are never dark-plumaged like immature Wandering Albatrosses. These two species have the largest wingspans of any bird; the largest ever recorded, that of a Wandering Albatross, was over 3.33 m.

The birds build their nests on the Otago Peninsula, and Campbell, Auckland and Chatham Islands and they pair for life. Individual nests are normally sited so far apart that one sitting bird can seldom see another. The single white, elongated egg is incubated by both parents and the chick is well guarded until it is too large to be attacked by skuas. The parents pay it brief visits and feed it with regurgitated plankton and their great white chick, which may weigh more than an adult, makes play nests or adds to the original. When fully fledged it leaves to spend the next six years at sea. Because of the long nesting period of about nine months the large albatrosses, unlike the smaller species, breed only every other year.

BLACK-BROWED MOLLYMAWK

ROYAL ALBATROSS

BLACK-BROWED MOLLYMAWK *Diomedea melanophris* 60 cm The adults of the New Zealand race *D.m.impavida* have honey-coloured eyes and nest on Campbell Island while the circumpolar race *D.m.melanophris* has dark eyes at all ages and nests on Antipodes and Macquarie Islands. This species frequently associates with Grey-headed Mollymawks. They make a characteristic sheep-like 'bah'. Unlike the larger albatrosses they do not depend upon the winds but fly into their nesting grounds on cliffs at tremendous speeds, turn into the wind using their feet and spread wings to brake, then drop on to the right spot. To take off they leap out and sail away on up-draughts. To make their nests of mud and straw they plaster on mud with their bills, trample the straw down with large webbed feet and by rotating their bodies form a hollow on the top. The nests are well drained and dry and the young excrete over the sides. The eggs are elongated and white with speckles at the larger end.

PRIONS *Pachyptila* spp. 25-30 cm Small petrels. Blue-grey above, white below, prions have a distinctive dark W on their backs, dark-tipped tail feathers and dark ear-coverts. They feed upon plankton near the sea's surface, straining water through lamelliae in their bills. Gregarious, they form dense flocks and breed in large warrens on New Zealand islands.

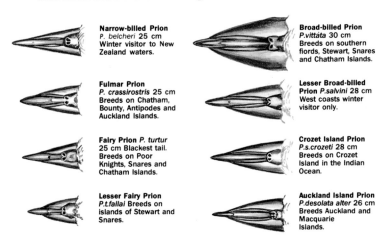

Narrow-billed Prion
P. belcheri 25 cm
Winter visitor to New Zealand waters.

Broad-billed Prion
P.vittäta 30 cm
Breeds on southern fiords, Stewart, Snares and Chatham Islands.

Fulmar Prion
P. crassirostris 25 cm
Breeds on Chatham, Bounty, Antipodes and Auckland Islands.

Lesser Broad-billed Prion *P.salvini* 28 cm
West coasts winter visitor only.

Fairy Prion *P. turtur*
25 cm Blackest tail.
Breeds on Poor Knights, Snares and Chatham Islands.

Crozet Island Prion
P.s.crozeti 28 cm
Breeds on Crozet Island in the Indian Ocean.

Lesser Fairy Prion
P.t.fallai Breeds on islands of Stewart and Snares.

Auckland Island Prion
P.desolata alter 26 cm
Breeds Auckland and Macquarie Islands.

ANTARCTIC FULMAR *Fulmarus glacialoides* 43 cm This fulmar is slightly larger and paler than its northern counterpart and has a pinkish horn-coloured bill and pale flesh-coloured feet. A regular visitor along the coasts of the main islands, its numbers have significantly increased since 1969. It breeds south of the Antarctic Circle.

BLUE PETREL *Halobaena caerulea* 30 cm Very like a prion, blue-grey above and white below with an inverted W across the wings, but with a white tail tip, this petrel is found on Macquarie Island throughout the breeding season. It is thought to breed there or in places in the South Atlantic and Indian Oceans. It is probably circumpolar in the southern hemisphere.

CAPE PIGEON *Daption capense* 40 cm Flocks of this strikingly-patterned black and white bird will visit inshore waters scavenging for offal. It makes harsh cackles at sea and softer calls on its nest on inaccessible ledges. It breeds as far north as Snares Island and also on most sub-antarctic islands. It lays one white egg which both parents guard well.

GIANT PETREL There are two species, both 65 cm The northern form, *Macronectes halli*, is dull brown with lighter face and horn-coloured bill, the southern *M.giganteus* is more variable with a greenish bill and has a white phase. Large flocks scavenge around whaling stations and coastal slaughterhouses, giving hoarse, wheezy croaks. *M.halli* breeds on Chatham, Stewart, Snares, Auckland, Campbell, Antipodes and Macquarie Islands, *M.giganteus* only on Macquarie Island.

ANTARCTIC FULMAR

BLUE PETREL

Black-
bellied
Storm
Petrel

PRIONS

CAPE PIGEON

GIANT PETREL

immature

31

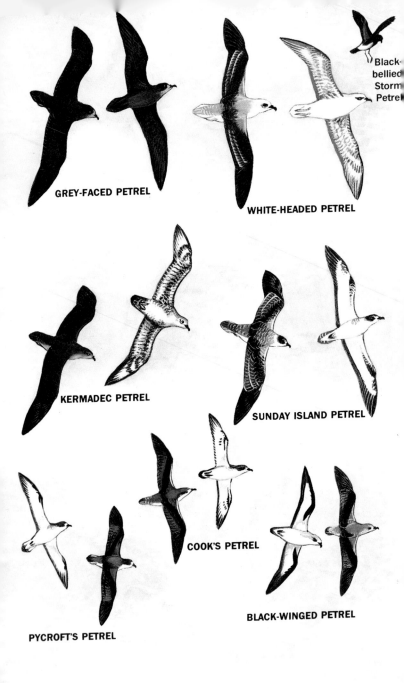

GREY-FACED PETREL

WHITE-HEADED PETREL

Black-bellied Storm Petrel

KERMADEC PETREL

SUNDAY ISLAND PETREL

PYCROFT'S PETREL

COOK'S PETREL

BLACK-WINGED PETREL

GREY-FACED PETREL *Pterodroma macroptera* 41 cm The 'mutton-bird' of the North Island Maoris is very dark with grey forehead, face and throat and has a strong, rapid, wheeling flight. It is a winter breeder on most offshore islands and mainland cliffs from Three Kings to North Taranaki and East Cape. Like other petrels its whistling, guttural calls are heard only at the breeding sites.

WHITE-HEADED PETREL *Pterodroma lessoni* 45 cm A light-coloured bird with dark wings, a dark line through the eye and a white head. This bird is common in the seas south of New Zealand. In winter it is a frequent casualty on beaches of the North Island's west coast. It breeds on Auckland, Antipodes and Macquarie Islands where its deep purring call may be heard.

KERMADEC PETREL *Pterodroma neglecta* 38 cm This petrel has three forms, all dark-winged. The *light* bases to the primaries show when the wings are spread. The light form resembles a smaller White-headed Petrel and the intermediate form is mottled. It is a petrel which ranges in subtropical waters and breeds in the New Zealand region on several islands of the Kermadec group.

SUNDAY ISLAND PETREL *Pterodroma cervicalis* 43 cm This petrel is very different from all others in the region, having a black cap and white collar. It is found near the Kermadecs and breeds in great numbers on Macauley Island. It returns to breed in October, lays eggs in December and its young are ready to fly by late May and June.

PYCROFT'S PETREL *Pterodroma pycrofti* 28 cm It has a proportionately longer tail and shorter bill and wings than Cook's Petrel, and its oceanic range is unknown. It breeds on the forested islands of Hen and Chickens, Poor Knights and Red Mercury, where it recently has been discovered. It has a short laying season and makes a variety of calls, buzzes or croons, not unlike those of Cook's Petrel.

COOK'S PETREL *Pterodroma cooki* 30 cm The wheeling flight of this bird shows first white underparts then grey upperparts with the dark inverted W across the wings. It breeds on Little and Great Barrier and Codfish Isles and has an astonishing variety of calls.

BLACK-WINGED PETREL *Pterodroma nigripennis* 30 cm Boldly patterned black on white underwings, white axillaries (like Cook's and unlike the Chatham Island, which has black) identify this petrel. It calls night and day as it flies over its breeding grounds which are mainly on the Poor Knights, Chatham and Norfolk Islands. It is the most common petrel to fly aboard ships in mid-Pacific and pairs indulge in spirited chases.

Black-
bellied
Storm
Petrel

WHITE-
CHINNED
PETREL

WESTLAND
BLACK
PETREL

GREY PETREL

BLACK PETREL

SOOTY SHEARWATER

LITTLE SHEARWATER

GREY PETREL *Procellaria cinerea* 48 cm Grey under-wing coverts are the field characteristic of this circumpolar breeder of the southern seas. Only occasionally seen off the main coasts, it keeps to cooler waters. Large numbers breed on Antipodes and in smaller numbers on Campbell Islands.

WHITE-CHINNED PETREL *Procellaria aequinoctialis steadi* 51 cm A large, black cold-water-haunting petrel with variable white patches on its chin. Its clackings from its burrow have earned it the name 'shoemaker'. Rare along main coasts, it breeds on Macquarie, Campbell, Antipodes and Auckland Islands.

WESTLAND BLACK PETREL *Procellaria westlandica* 51 cm Very like the Black Petrel with a generally yellowish bill, this bird breeds on coastal ranges one kilometre inland. A crescendo of shrieks develops at its breeding site at dusk and intermittent calls continue until the start of the pre-dawn chorus.

BLACK PETREL *Procellaria parkinsoni* 43 cm Smaller than the Westland and with an ivory bill (bluish-grey in immatures) the Black breeds inland on bush-clad mountain tops at Little and Great Barrier Islands. It arrives silently at breeding sites then makes staccato clack-clacks and hisses. Migratory, it occurs as a non-breeder around the Galapagos Islands.

SOOTY SHEARWATER *Puffinus griseus* 43 cm A browny-grey bird with conspicuous silvery flashes from its underwing coverts in flight. Many thousands of young birds are collected as food on some islands off Stewart Island. Only Maoris belonging to the tribes from those islands are allowed to collect these muttonbirds.

LITTLE SHEARWATER *Puffinus assimilis* 30 cm The smallest New Zealand shearwater, black above, pure white below. Scattered colonies breed in wooded terrain on several islands from the Kermadecs to the Auckland Islands.

GREY PETREL

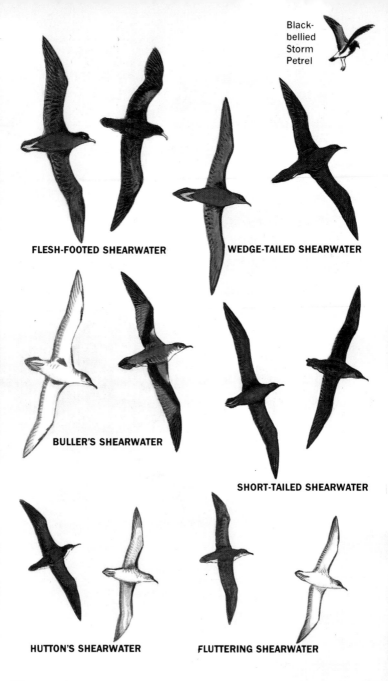

Black-bellied Storm Petrel

FLESH-FOOTED SHEARWATER

WEDGE-TAILED SHEARWATER

BULLER'S SHEARWATER

SHORT-TAILED SHEARWATER

HUTTON'S SHEARWATER

FLUTTERING SHEARWATER

FLESH-FOOTED SHEARWATER *Puffinus carneipes* 46 cm A more compactly built bird than other New Zealand shearwaters, this is most likely to be confused with the Black Petrel, but has pale feet. Nestlings have grey down and a first plumage similar to the adult. It breeds from the Hen and Chicken Islands to Cook Strait and ranges south as far as the Chathams and seas off New Zealand coasts at that latitude. Its variety of calls and mews are heard on shore.

WEDGE-TAILED SHEARWATER *Puffinus pacificus* 46 cm Its slender dark bill and long wedge tail distinguish this shearwater from the Flesh-footed. It has two phases: in the Kermadecs the breeding population is dark while the white-breasted form breeds on islands north of the Equator and islands off Western Australia. Like the Flesh-footed it has a variety of weird calls which sound like fighting, snarling cats.

BULLER'S SHEARWATER *Puffinus bulleri* 46 cm This large bird has a wedge-shaped tail but is greyer than the preceding species, with white underparts, flesh-coloured feet and a dark bill. A distinctive dark W across the wings is broken by grey upper-tail coverts. Its only known breeding area is at Poor Knights Islands, whence it disperses to the Banks Peninsula and west Cook Strait, migrating to the Pacific in winter. Mews and cackling noises may be heard at its breeding sites.

SHORT-TAILED SHEARWATER *Puffinus tenuirostris* 35 cm This, the Tasman 'muttonbird', is like the Sooty Shearwater but smaller with a relatively smaller bill and no pale underwing areas. It breeds in burrows on islands in the Bass Strait and occurs regularly in the outer waters of the Hauraki Gulf and the Bay of Plenty. The young are fed at increasingly longer intervals until they exceed the adult weight but remain in the burrows until fully fledged.

HUTTON'S SHEARWATER *Puffinus huttoni* 36 cm This species generally has duskier feathers under the wings and is darker than the Fluttering Shearwater. It breeds, at 1000 m and above, only in the Seaward Kaikouras and is abundant in Cook Strait and off the east coast of the South Island. 'Wrecked' birds on their first flight are occasionally found on the west coast of Auckland. It makes deeper and harsher calls than the Fluttering.

FLUTTERING SHEARWATER *Puffinus gavia* 33 cm This is a small shearwater, brown above with a faint suggestion of collar and breast patch on white undersides, and with very white underwings. It spends a lot of time resting on the water or skimming over the sea with rapid wing beats, in rough weather flying in rising and falling glides. It breeds on islands from Three Kings to the Cook Strait, feeding near shore and ranging to eastern Australian seaboards. It makes a very loud noise for such a small bird.

WHITE-FACED STORM PETREL *Pelagadroma marina* 20 cm This is the only storm petrel which is common in coastal waters. It will sometimes rest high on calm water with wings and tail held at a sharp angle. After dark, twittering is heard from its dense breeding colonies on many islands from the Kermadecs to the Auckland Islands, including a large colony on Chatham. It is prey to skuas, gulls and harriers.

BLACK-BELLIED STORM PETREL *Fregetta tropica* 20 cm Its white flanks and zigzag flight help to distinguish this species from Wilson's Storm Petrel which has a white rump, black undersides and a less erratic flight. It is a circumpolar species breeding on many sub-antarctic islands. (It has been added to other petrel/shearwater plates to show scale.)

GREY-BACKED STORM PETREL *Garrodia nereis* 18 cm This small, circumpolar petrel with *no* white on the rump breeds on many sub-antarctic islands. Its rat-hole-like burrows are found in tussock vegetation, but breeding is prevented on islands inhabited by Norway rats. Its remains have been found in castings of skuas.

DIVING PETRELS are specialised birds, confined to the southern hemisphere. Stocky, black above and white below, they resemble the auks of the northern hemisphere. They skim over the sea in rapid, whirring flight and frequently dive below the surface. Using feet and powerful wings they swim underwater, emerge and continue their flight.

NORTHERN DIVING PETREL *Pelacanoides urinatrix* 20 cm Three subspecies are all burrow breeders on offshore islands. The northern form *P.u.urinatrix* breeds on islands from the Three Kings to Foveaux Strait. The somewhat smaller *P.u.chathamensis* breeds on Chatham, Solander and Stewart Islands and the Snares.

The sub-antarctic form, *Pelacanoides urinatrix exsul,* breeds on islands such as Auckland and Macquarie. It has a wider-based bill and generally more pronounced speckles on its breast.

SOUTH GEORGIAN DIVING PETREL *Pelacanoides georgicus* 17 cm Rare in New Zealand waters, breeding on Codfish Islands, Foveaux Strait and possibly still on Auckland Islands, its range is circumpolar. It may be more pelagic than other diving petrels.

BLACK-BELLIED STORM PETREL

WHITE-FACED STORM PETREL

GREY-BACKED STORM PETREL

DIVING PETREL

39

immature

immature

immature

AUSTRALIAN GANNET

AUSTRALIAN GANNET *Sula bassana serrator* 91 cm Birds of temperate waters, gannets make spectacular vertical dives into the sea for fish. They breed in colonies numbering thousands, the most famous at Cape Kidnappers. Immatures are speckled brown, the single chicks, first black and naked, become white and fluffy.

MASKED BOOBY *Sula dactylatra* 86 cm Boobies are birds of tropical waters, the Masked seldom ranging south of the Kermadecs. Its dark tail, broad wing bands and yellow bill are characteristic. Immatures are mottled brown above with dark heads and necks. Normally two eggs are laid but only one chick reared.

BROWN BOOBY *Sula leucogaster* 74 cm This chocolate-brown Booby with white underwing coverts and belly and pale yellow feet probably visits northern New Zealand waters every summer. Immature birds are identified by their wing pattern, brown belly and dark brown breast.

immature

immature

MASKED BOOBY

BROWN BOOBY

immature

RED-TAILED TROPIC BIRD

RED-TAILED TROPIC BIRD *Phaethon rubricauda* 46 cm (excluding two central tail feathers) Immatures have black bills and more heavily marked plumage before developing the characteristic red bill and long tail. They breed on Norfolk and Kermadec Islands. White-tailed Tropic Birds *P. lepturus*, 36 cm, also occasionally straggle to New Zealand waters.

immature

LITTLE SHAG

LITTLE BLACK SHAG

PIED SHAG

1st year

BLACK SHAG

42

PIED SHAG *Phalocrocorax varius* 81 cm Restricted to the warmer parts of New Zealand and discontinuous in range, these shags are most plentiful on northern coasts and offshore islands, rare inland. A typical colony is found in trees, especially Pohutukawas, on exposed sea cliffs, some in trees near coastal lakes. They eat mostly estuarine fish and make deep croaks and wheezy calls. The clutch is 2-4. Immatures are browner above with occasional brown feathers on white underparts.

BLACK SHAG *Phalacrocorax carbo* 88 cm Colour and facial markings are field characteristics of this shag while the white feathers on neck and thighs are seasonal. Females are smaller. They feed, mostly inland, on main and Chatham Islands, straggling to Campbell and Macquarie. In autumn and early winter flocks numbering hundreds form, feeding and diving in sheltered tidal waters. They make hoarse croaks and wheezy whistling notes. The clutch is 3-4.

LITTLE SHAG *Phalacrocorax melanoleucos brevirostris* 25 cm A variable species, most abundant in its white-throated form. It is similar to the Little Black Shag in size but has a relatively shorter tail and a short stout bill. Most immatures are all black with yellow bills but immature pieds are dirty white below. They nest in trees, lay 3-4 eggs and chicks have white tufts on black down. They wheeze and coo.

LITTLE BLACK SHAG *Phalacrocorax sulcirostris* 61 cm A small, slim, all-black bird with a comparatively long tail and long, slender, black bill. It is probably increasing in the north of the North Island but is rare in the South Island. It hunts in packs, rounding up fish, moves north in winter and nests later than other shags in Rangaunu Bay and the Bay of Plenty. It lays 2-5 eggs. Immatures are duller.

Pied Shags

KING SHAG *Leucocarbo carunculatus carunculatus* 76 cm Of oceanic habitat, this shag feeds on bottom and weed-living fish and crustacea. Its large nests, built of seaweeds, are closely spaced on rocky islets and it lays 3 eggs. Immatures are dull brown above. Its voice is a croak.

STEWART ISLAND SHAG *Leucocarbo carunculatus chalconotus* 68 cm Resembling the King Shag but without white on scapulars, this shag has two colour phases. It is found at coastal Otago, Foveaux Strait and Stewart Island.

CHATHAM ISLAND SHAG *Leucocarbo carunculatus onslowi* 63 cm Sleek, glossy, with bright face colours, this shag is restricted to its name island.

BOUNTY ISLAND SHAG *Leucocarbo campbelli ranfurlyi* 71 cm Restricted to its name island this shag has no caruncles, a bright red face, a slight dorsal patch and makes nests of vegetation and guano on rocky ledges.

AUCKLAND ISLAND SHAG *Leucocarbo campbelli colensoi* 63 cm Resembling the previous shag, the dark throat feathers of this numerous species meet in some birds. Nests are like other shags and it lays 3 eggs.

CAMPBELL ISLAND SHAG *Leucocarbo campbelli campbelli* 63 cm Restricted to its island group this less numerous shag is darker and less variable than the Auckland Island and its dark throat feathers always meet. Immatures are dull brown with mottled throats. Nests like other shags, lays 3 eggs.

MACQUARIE ISLAND SHAG *Leucocarbo albiventer purpurascens* 73 cm Resembling the two preceding species, but with a royal blue gloss, this shag has no white scapulars or dorsal patch but more on the face, beginning at the gape not the lower mandibles. Restricted to Macquarie, compact colonies nest on low rocks and coastal ledges. Immatures brown above, white below.

SPOTTED SHAG *Stictocarbo punctatus* 73 cm Locally common in North Island, abundant in South Island, this shag wears non-breeding dress for most of the year. Duller immatures pass through many stages to full adult plumage. Nests on steep cliff faces.

PITT ISLAND SHAG *Stictocarbo punctatus featherstoni* 63 cm Restricted to the Chathams and most numerous south of Pitt Strait, this shag is darker than the Spotted and has no white neck stripes. Nests on rock ledges.

SPOTTED SHAG

winter

breeding

PITT ISLAND SHAG

winter

breeding

CHATHAM ISLAND SHAG

black phase

KING SHAG

STEWART ISLAND SHAG

CAMPBELL ISLAND SHAG

AUCKLAND ISLAND SHAG

BOUNTY ISLAND SHAG

MACQUARIE ISLAND SHAG

immature

45

WHITE-FACED HERON *Ardea novaehollandiae* 66 cm This Australian species is the most plentiful heron in New Zealand. Colonization of farm dams by Australian green frogs has helped its dispersion. It has a strong leisurely flight, gaining height quickly, and often perches on posts with its head tucked in. It makes guttural grunts both on the wing and on arrival at its nest. It lays a clutch of 3-5 matt blue-green eggs.

REEF HERON *Egretta sacra* 66 cm Found near tidelines and, sparsely, on rocky coasts, this heron with its crouching gait and heavy bill is usually solitary but forms small flocks in northern harbours. It is absent from sandy beaches and commonest north of the Bay of Plenty. It generally flies low over the water, makes guttural croaks and nests, sometimes with other pairs, in caves. The clutch is of 2-3 eggs.

LITTLE EGRET *Egretta garzetta immaculata* 56 cm When breeding this heron has two narrow-pointed plumes on its head and others on breast and back. Fast wing beats enable it to gain height quickly. It is cosmopolitan, recorded from many coastal lakes and estuaries but rare inland. It is seldom found in groups larger than five and is often solitary although it associates quite happily with other herons or large waders. It may be harrassed by gulls.

Reef Heron

WHITE-FACED HERON

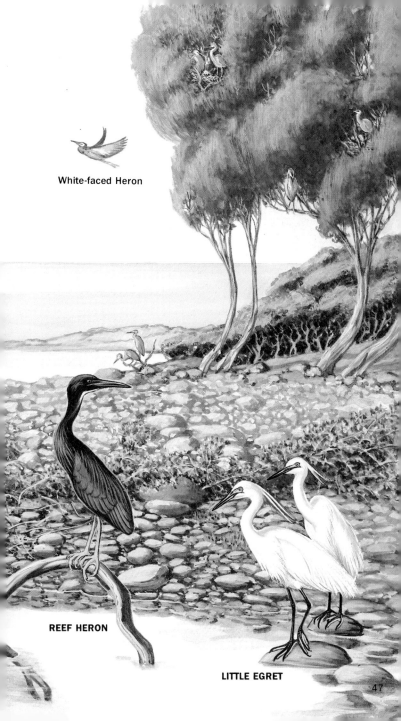

White-faced Heron

REEF HERON

LITTLE EGRET

47

ROYAL SPOONBILL *Platalea regia* 78 cm Spoonbills are large heron-like birds with slightly curved, black spatulate bills which they sweep from side to side, moving forward as they feed. Immatures have brown on their primaries. Spoonbills have a strong, gliding, soaring flight with the head extended, unlike herons, and they haunt waters of tidal creeks. They lay 3–4 white eggs blotched with brown.

GLOSSY IBIS *Plegadis falcinellus* 56 cm In the distance the glossy purplish-green-bronze Ibis appears black. It flies with neck and feet extended and a faster wing beat than herons or egrets, gains height quickly and often glides. In flocks Ibis make grunting noises. After breeding colonies disperse widely. They visit from Australia when conditions of prolonged drought in the big river swamps force them to find new feeding grounds. Then, if food is plentiful, they may remain for weeks. They eat tadpoles, feeding busily like starlings.

ROYAL SPOONBILL

GLOSSY IBIS

WHITE HERON *Egretta alba modesta* 91 cm This elegant pure white heron, plumed in its breeding dress, has a characteristic double kink in the neck. The upper parts of the legs are sometimes yellowish. Few lakes, estuaries or coastal lagoons are without this cosmopolitan species which disperses throughout the country after breeding near Okarito, in Kahikatea swamp. They nest in the crowns of tree-ferns, in Kowhai or Kamahi, which they share with Little Shags. They lay 3–5 bluish-green eggs.

AUSTRALASIAN BITTERN *Botaurus stellaris poiciloptilus* 71 cm Fairly widely distributed, bitterns 'pretend' to be reeds. They point their bills skywards and look straight at the watcher with both eyes. They fly on broad, rounded wings with their heads tucked in like herons. Seldom seen as it creeps through reeds and rushes, the male 'booms' resonantly during the mating season (August–February). In autumn young birds are often flushed on salt marshes. The female builds a firm platform of reeds (preferably Raupo surrounded by water) on which she lays 3–5 greenish-cream eggs and incubates them alone.

WHITE HERON **AUSTRALASIAN BITTERN**

immature

BLACK SWAN

MUTE SWAN

CANADA GO

50

MUTE SWAN *Cygnus olor* 150 cm Introduced from England for ornamental purposes the Mute swan is still semi-domestic but has established breeding populations on Ellesmere and other lakes. Largest of the waterfowl, it is pure white and flies with the neck extended (unlike herons). In spring the knob on the bill of the male enlarges greatly. This swan's trumpeting call is seldom heard but it snorts and hisses if annoyed. It builds a vast nest on the water's edge and lays 5-7 off-white eggs. The cygnets are downy at first, becoming greyish above and white below.

BLACK SWAN *Cygnus atratus* 100 cm Introduced from Australia for ornamental purposes this swan is now so widespread on lakes and estuaries that its numbers sometimes need reducing. It has white flight feathers but those of the dark ashy-brown immature birds have black tips. It builds large mound nests on rivers, or, in colonies, on lake shores where it may or may not be surrounded by vegetation. It whistles if disturbed and also makes a musical crooning sound. The 4-7 eggs are greenish-white.

CANADA GOOSE *Branta canadensis* 100 cm This North American goose was introduced for game purposes and is now abundant in Canterbury and North Otago where it breeds mostly in high, grassy mountain valleys, some birds migrating to Lake Ellesmere in winter. Few breed in the North Island but stragglers appear in most districts. It has white cheeks and undertail feathers which are conspicuous on water. It gives a double honk on water or wing and has a high-pitched breeding call. It makes a mound nest with a wide view and lays 2-11 creamy-white eggs. The young have yellowish down with brown marks above.

PARADISE SHELDUCK *Tadorna variegata* 63 cm
The Shelduck's heavy build and short neck prevents confusion with larger geese or smaller duck. They are usually found in pairs or family groups and easily adapt to hill pastures, rearing their young in stock ponds. The white wing-coverts and green speculum are visible in flight and the female's white head is conspicuous. They are found all over the main islands, some in large numbers. Their high-pitched call is carrying. Nests are lined with down, in depressions on the ground or up to 6 m up in trees, log piles or haystacks. They lay 8-12 white eggs.

GREY DUCK *Anas superciliosa* 55 cm Similar to female Mallards, except for more pronounced striped pattern on the face. Both sexes look the same, with a green speculum. Preferring cover, they avoid farmlands, concealing their dry-grass and down-lined nests in hollows and forks of trees away from water. The clutch of eggs numbers 10. Their calls are similar to the Mallard's.

MALLARD *Anas platyrhynchos* 58 cm Introduced first from Britain, then from the United States, Mallard were intensively bred and then released. They have a fast take-off and irregular flight. They have a purple-blue speculum edged by white bars. In captivity Mallard hybridize with Grey Duck but rarely do so in the wild, where they compete for food. Mallard are more numerous in settled land. They nest in hollows of trees and tree forks and in long grass, similar sites to those of the Grey Duck, and are rarely far away from water. They continually add down as they incubate their 10-15 whitish eggs. They have a variety of harsh and soft quacks.

Hybrid Grey Duck and Mallard

♀ immature

♀

PARADISE SHELDUCK

♂

GREY DUCK

MALLARD

♂

♀

NEW ZEALAND SHOVELER *Anas rhynchotis variegata* 48 cm The Shoveler is widely spread, probably increasing in number, and readily colonizes lakes up to 700 m above sea level, new ponds and dams. A dumpier bird than the Mallard or Grey Duck, it has a much shorter neck than either and flies swiftly with abrupt turns. It feeds largely on aquatic creatures and seeds and does not graze on pastures like the Grey Duck. The male makes a muted 'clonk' at dusk and if disturbed. Shovelers nest in open grassy sites near water and lay 9-13 bluish-white eggs.

GREY TEAL *Anas gibberifrons* 43 cm Smaller than the Grey Duck, with no head stripes, greyer than the female Mallard and with a smaller head than the Shoveler, the Grey Teal has very fast wing beats, the white-fronted green speculum being prominent in flight. A flock will wheel rapidly. Self-introduced from Australia it is established in many areas, spreading more each year. It makes a rapid 'cuck, cuck, cuck' and soft 'eep' to its young. Its usually down-lined nest is near water, in vegetation or the tops of 'niggerhead' and tree-forks. It lays 3-9 dark cream eggs.

BROWN TEAL *Anas aucklandica chlorotis* 48 cm Brown Teal were once common in swampy streams, ponds and sheltered tidal creeks, coming out to feed at night. Large numbers remain on Great Barrier Islands and there are a few other small groups scattered around, but early Europeans took them for food, and drained the swamps so that they are now rare. They fly well, though seldom, dive often and may rest and feed on bull-kelp on sheltered coasts. The Brown Teal has a low 'quark' and a high-pitched pipe. Its down-lined nest is hidden in grass near water. It lays 5-7 cream eggs.

AUCKLAND ISLAND TEAL *Anas aucklandica aucklandica* 43 cm A nocturnal feeder on kelp in sheltered coastal locations this flightless duck is found in the Auckland Islands, nesting on the smaller islets. Cats probably keep it off the main island. It uses its wings as climbing aids. The speculum and wing-bars show little more than a brownish gloss. Its voice is like the Brown Teal's. It lines its nest with grass and down, hides it under vegetation and lays 3-5 cream eggs.

NEW ZEALAND SHOVELER

GREY TEAL

BROWN TEAL

AUCKLAND ISLAND TEAL

BLUE DUCK *Hymenolaimus malacorhynchos* 53 cm Most active at dusk, Blue Duck live in pairs or family groups on turbulent mountain streams in both islands. They take surface insects but obtain much food by diving, even in the swiftest currents, and searching the stream bed for its abundant insect life. Although they are strong fliers they prefer escaping by diving and swimming away. Their tameness led to depletion but with protection they are now increasing. The male makes a shrill hoarse 'Whio' — its Maori name; the female cries 'creck' or 'rattles'. Their nests, mud-lined and well-hidden in vegetation, are often on steep stream banks. They lay 4-6 creamy-white eggs.

NEW ZEALAND SCAUP *Aythya novaeseelandiae* 40 cm This duck is found in mountain lakes, coastal ponds, sand-dune lakes and other lakes of both islands. Not numerous, because of past habitat destruction and uncontrolled shooting, it has now colonised some North Island hydro-lakes and artificial ponds and increased its numbers. The male whistles quietly, the brown-eyed female has a quiet quack. They probably do not breed until at least two years old. The grass- and down-lined nests are close to water, hidden in thick vegetation. The clutch is 5-8 creamy-white eggs and the young can dive to considerable depths shortly after hatching.

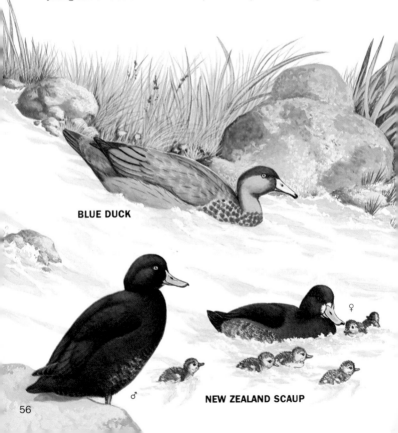

BLUE DUCK

♂

NEW ZEALAND SCAUP

♀

NEW ZEALAND DABCHICK *Podiceps rufopectus* 28 cm This little grebe has a fluffy white rear and is an expert diver. Sedentary, it is found widely in sand-dune pools and volcanic plateau lakes in the North Island up to 900 m above sea level. It colonises new dams and reservoirs, avoiding eel-infested shallow lakes. It makes a sibilant 'wee-e-ee' and pairs chatter gutturally. Its bulky, though flimsy, nest, sometimes on a solid base, is of water-logged vegetation anchored to reeds or overhead branches. The 2-3 white eggs are covered with weed when the bird leaves the nest and quickly become stained yellowish-brown. Quick to enter the water after hatching, the young often ride on their parents' backs.

CRESTED GREBE *Podiceps cristatus australis* 50 cm This grebe lives in lowland and subalpine lakes in the South Island and is occasionally found along coasts and estuaries. Very rarely found in the North Island. Shy and seldom heard. When disturbed or near its nest it makes hoarse wailing cries. In a remarkable courtship display the pair swim towards each other, shaking their heads, rise upright and stand body to body. Nests, sometimes on land, are of floating vegetation anchored to reeds or overhanging branches. A clutch of 3-5 bluish eggs is laid. The young swim on hatching but, tiring easily, frequently ride their parents' backs.

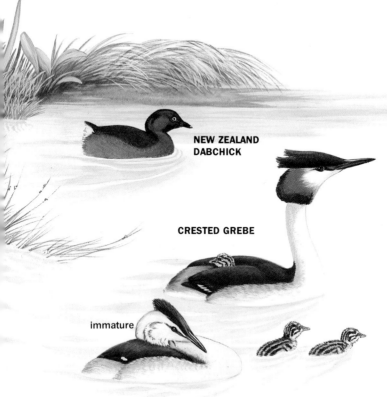

NEW ZEALAND
DABCHICK

CRESTED GREBE

immature

immature

♂

♀

AUSTRALIAN HARRIER

AUSTRALIAN HARRIER *Circus approximans gouldi* 63 cm Adult female birds of prey are generally larger and heavier than adult males; the New Zealand representatives are no exception. Farmers opening up the country increased the Harrier's food supply and now, except in heavily forested areas, it is commonly seen quartering the ground in leisurely flight, looking for animals killed on the roads or dead sheep. It also wades into shallow water after frogs. It is often mobbed by flocks of magpies and starlings and roosts communally in winter. Mewing and squealing in courtship flights, the male may pass food to the female who turns her back and takes it with her feet. Nests are built in swamps or scrub and 2-7 white eggs are laid.

NANKEEN KESTREL

♂

♀

♂

Chaffinch

immature
♀

NEW ZEALAND FALCON

♂

NANKEEN KESTREL *Falco cenchroides* 33 cm
On west coasts in autumn it is worth watching
for this kestrel, a rare straggler from Australia.
The female has a rufous tail, the male a grey
tail and rump. A typical kestrel, it hovers head
into the wind and drops on its prey of small
mammals, lizards and insects. It has bred on
Norfolk Island and it is to be hoped may one
day breed in New Zealand.

NEW ZEALAND FALCON *Falco novaeseelandiae* 45 cm This falcon has shorter wings than
many others. It preys largely on birds and is
very intolerant of intruders. Immatures invari-
ably have blue-grey ceres and feet and darker
plumage than adults and they may visit sub-
urban areas. Common in the south back-
country, it is rare north of Rotorua, thriving on
the Auckland Islands. It nests on cliff ledges
or, in steep bush, on the ground, more rarely
in trees, and lays 2-4 red-brown blotched
eggs.

CHUKOR

CHUKOR *Alectoris chukar* 33 cm
Introduced from Asia, the Chukor is
well established in high country (up
to 1800 m) from Nelson to Otago.
Males have spurs on their legs. The
striped flanks are puffed out over
drooping wings in display. It lives in
coveys, feeding on roots, seeds
and insects and forms larger flocks
in autumn. The 10-18 greyish-
brown freckled eggs are incubated
by the female and newly-hatched
chicks walk and run as soon as
they are dry.

GREY PARTRIDGE *Perdix perdix* 30 cm The horseshoe on the male's breast
is darkish, faint on the female's and absent in the young. Partridges live in
coveys, squatting at approaching danger then, when almost underfoot,
'explode' into glide-broken flight. Their calls are harsh 'kirrick, kirricks'. They
nest on the ground, covering each egg with dead leaves until the clutch of
9-20 is complete. The chicks leave the nest within hours, fly at 16 days and
feed on insects before becoming largely vegetarian.

PHEASANT *Phasianus colchicus* male 80 cm, female 60 cm Although they
roost in trees, pheasants spend most of the time on the ground, feeding on
insects and plant matter and, though widely released, prefer northern
coastal scrub. The cock is polygamous and aggressive when breeding. He
jumps up and down in front of rivals with much wing flapping and his harsh
'kok, kok' persists at daybreak. Preferring to run for cover, pheasants 'explode' and take flight like partridges. They lay 10-15 olive eggs in a grass-
lined scrape in the ground. The chicks can fly when two weeks old.

GREY PARTRIDGE

♂

♀

♀

PHEASANT

♂

61

HELMETED GUINEA FOWL

BOBWHITE
QUAIL

♂

♀

CALIFORNIA QUAIL

♂

♀

62

HELMETED GUINEA FOWL *Numida meleagris* 63 cm This gregarious, flocking bird, introduced from European domestic stock, is wild in some areas of New Zealand but seldom seen. Sometimes only the odd feather indicates its presence. It likes rough country with good cover and feeds on the ground. It gives a harsh cackle. Adult birds run away but if they have young with them will erupt into flight, skim the ground and drop in cover. The species makes a scrape in the ground and lays 7–12 eggs. Chicks retain hairy black-streaked down for six weeks.

BOBWHITE QUAIL *Colinus virginianus* 23 cm These quail resemble very small partridges and the male has a conspicuous white throat. Introduced from North America, they may survive in two localities in northern Hawke's Bay. They form coveys in the off-season and roost in outward-facing circles on weedy open ground. They eat plants and insects. Males fight until pairs are formed, feed the females in courtship and give the musical 'Bobwhite' call from post or branch. They lay 7–28 white eggs in cover and the young fly within a week of hatching.

CALIFORNIA QUAIL *Lophortyx californica* 25 cm A plump and stocky bird, the male having a distinct plume on the head, California Quail are spread widely through main and offshore islands. They post sentinels and feed on plants and insects in scrub and cultivated land. The coveys disperse in winter. They have many calls, including a triple which starlings imitate, and prefer to run for cover, although they have a fast, gliding flight. They nest near thick cover in a hollow in the ground and lay 9–16 creamy-white eggs with brown spots.

♀

BROWN QUAIL

♂

BROWN QUAIL *Synoicus ypsilophorus* 18 cm Small, plump, crouching birds, the females slightly larger than the males, Brown Quail make short flights. They were introduced from Australia but probably colonised naturally also and may be found feeding on plants and insects in the swamps, salt-marsh edges and roadside scrub of the northern North Island and some offshore islands. They are scarce in southern areas. They make a variety of calls from one of which, 'Moreete', they get their Aborigine name. They nest in grass-lined hollows and lay 1–12 dull, white-brown speckled eggs.

PEAFOWL ♀

TURKEY ♀

Saddlebacks

TURKEY

♂

PEAFOWL

♂

PEAFOWL *Pavo cristatus* 86 cm Peafowl were introduced in 1843 and feral populations exist from Kaipara to Wanganui and Hawke's Bay. They live in small groups of one male and several females and feed on the ground on seeds, fruit and plants and small animals. The female lays her 3-5 eggs in a well-hidden hollow in the ground. The male's splendid display is not of tail feathers but of elongated tail coverts. The introduction of such exotic birds has been a threat to New Zealand's native species, particularly those which feed on the ground and nest only a little above it, e.g. the Saddleback.

TURKEY *Meleagris gallopavo* 86 cm Male turkeys are larger than females, weighing up to 10 kilograms, and have more wattles on their heads. Introduced before 1890, turkeys have become feral in some districts. Their diet is almost entirely vegetarian: seeds, berries, fruit and nuts are ground down in a very powerful gizzard. At night they roost in trees. The hen lays up to 15 eggs which she incubates herself, the polygamous male taking no part in rearing the young. Young birds develop quickly. They can fly within two weeks of hatching, even though they are less than half the adult size.

immature

MARSH CRAKE

SPOTLESS CRAKE

BANDED RAIL

AUCKLAND ISLAND RAIL *Rallus pectoralis muelleri* 21 cm This rail, which may still survive on Adams and Ewing Islands, makes metallic 'creeks' and the typical rail grunt and double 'kek kek'. Its nest has never been found in New Zealand but it probably makes a grass cup in a swamp and lays 4-6 spotted eggs, like the related Australian Water Rail.

AUCKLAND ISLAND RAIL

MARSH CRAKE *Porzana pusilla affinis* 18 cm Marsh Crakes are shy and secretive with low, rapid flight when flushed. Widely spread, but nowhere common since they are easy prey to vermin, they inhabit the swamps and reed-edged lakes of both main islands, feeding on molluscs and water plants. They have sharp calls and rapid alarm trills. Their nests are open cups of leaves and stems in which 4-8 olive-brown, dark-streaked eggs are laid.

SPOTLESS CRAKE *Porzana tabuensis plumbea* 20 cm This elegant little rail flies for short distances only. An adaptable bird, it is found in raupo-filled swamps, grassland, forest floors and petrel burrows. A tree climber, it runs and swims well, diving to escape enemies. It squeaks, croons and scolds. A bulky nest of loose grass is built in which 2-3 pinkish-cream spotted eggs are laid.

BANDED RAIL *Rallus philippensis assimilis* 30 cm This rail is seldom seen but its varied calls are often heard. Secretive and semi-nocturnal, it flies for short distances with its legs dangling and flicks its tail when frightened. Adaptable to human settlement, it frequents coastal areas, feeding on small invertebrates. It builds a bowl-like nest at ground level in rushes or grass and lays 4-7 pinkish spotted eggs. The chicks have black down.

WEKA

WEKA *Gallirallus australis* 53 cm Four races are locally common; in East Cape and Kapiti, Marlborough to Fiordland, Arthur's Pass National Park and on Stewart Island. Introduced to Chatham Islands about 1905. This tame and inquisitive bird prefers forest verges and scrub. Omnivorous and a scavenger, it kills rats. A contact call is made by one bird 'cooeet', others joining in, and drumming noises are made while breeding. The nest is a well-hidden, grass-lined bowl and both sexes incubate the 3-6 eggs. Chicks have fluffy black down.

AUSTRALIAN COOT

immature

PUKEKO

immature

AUSTRALIAN COOT *Fulica atra australis* 38 cm The male is slightly larger than the female and juveniles are duller with no frontal shields. Coots often dive for weed and 'run' across the water when taking off in heavy flight. Their heads jerk back and forth as they swim. They make several sounds: 'cracks' and wood-chopping noises. Their numbers are increasing and they are found in lowland and sub-alpine reedy lakes, being most common in the North Island. They will travel long distances at night and flock in winter. The nest, sometimes solidly based, is made of willow rootlets and rushes and cradles 5-7 creamy-white, sparsely spotted eggs.

PUKEKO *Porphyrio melanotus* 51 cm The male is slightly larger than the female. This shy bird flicks its tail when nervous, showing white under-tail coverts. It flies strongly, its long legs dangling after a laboured take-off. It is widespread throughout swamps in New Zealand and the larger islands. It feeds on plants and small animals, in grassland, sometimes holding food in a foot. It has a variety of squeals, clicks and sighs and calls 'poo-koo-koo'. Often polygamous, it will build several bulky nests in swamps and lay 4-7 warmish-buff blotched eggs. Chicks have silver-tipped black down.

TAKAHE *Notornis mantelli* 63 cm This large, flightless gallinule pairs for life. Named from fossil bones it was discovered living in 1849 but later thought extinct until rediscovered in 1948. Now protected it lives in the tussock and snow-grass of the marshes and streams in the Murchison Range (at altitudes of 600-1,000 m) west of Lake Te Anau, leaving the valley for beech forest in winter. It has various alarm and contact calls. Vegetarian when adult, holding food down by foot, it will dig in moss for insect larvae to feed its downy black chicks for their first 2-3 weeks. It lays 1-4 dull-cream spotted eggs in a well-hidden grass bowl under snow-tussock.

TAKAHE

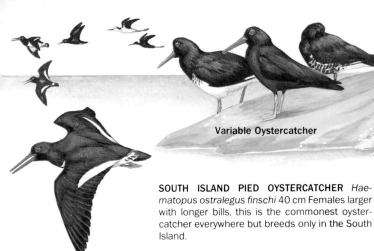

Variable Oystercatcher

South Island Pied
Oystercatcher

GREY PLOVER

breeding

SPUR-WINGED PLOVER

BLACK STILT

SOUTH ISLAND PIED OYSTERCATCHER *Haematopus ostralegus finschi* 40 cm Females larger with longer bills, this is the commonest oystercatcher everywhere but breeds only in the South Island.

VARIABLE OYSTERCATCHER *Haematopus unicolor* 48 cm Frequenting sandy beaches and breeding on the main islands and Stewart, the Variable shows less white than the Pied and also has a black form.

LEAST GOLDEN PLOVER *Pluvialis fulva* 25 cm The underside of its wings and its axillaries a uniform grey, this Plover is often seen with Turnstones.

GREY PLOVER *Pluvialis squatarola* 28 cm This Plover has black axillaries.

SPUR-WINGED PLOVER *Vanellus miles novaehollandiae* 38 cm Leisurely and heron-like in flight, with an upright walk and tip-toeing run, this Plover congregates in fields of root crops. Its wing spur is usually hidden.

PIED STILT *Himantopus himantopus leucocephalus* 38 cm Noisy and gregarious, often nesting in colonies, this is the commonest large breeding wader. In flight it trails its pink legs behind its tail.

BLACK STILT *Himantopus novaezealandiae* 38 cm Somewhat shorter-legged than the Pied, the Black Stilt is now rare. Scattered colonies breed in South Canterbury and North Otago.

VARIABLE OYSTERCATCHER

SOUTH ISLAND PIED OYSTERCATCHER

non-breeding

LEAST GOLDEN PLOVER

PIED STILT

SPUR-WINGED PLOVER

71

non-breeding

breeding

LARGE SAND DOTTEREL *Charadrius leschenaulti* 22 cm With a conspicuous white forehead and broadish wings which beat slowly, this summer visitor to northern inlets, Taranaki, Hawke's Bay, Farewell Spit and Southland lakes is found associating with other dotterels, wrybills and plovers and may overwinter.

BANDED DOTTEREL *Charadrius bicinctus* 18 cm Immature birds have speckly upper-parts, less white and no bands. Widespread and numerous, except in northern districts, Banded Dotterel flock off-season on tidal flats and pastures. They nest on lake and river shores, ploughed land, mountain slopes and, occasionally, beaches.

NEW ZEALAND DOTTEREL *Charadrius obscurus* 27 cm Moving more slowly than the Banded this Dotterel runs with a lowered head and has a strong gliding flight. Rather sedentary, it frequents ocean beaches, estuarine flats and nearby paddocks, ground nesting in the environs of Auckland, the Bay of Plenty, Stewart Island and Southland.

BLACK-FRONTED DOTTEREL *Charadrius melanops* 18 cm A fast runner with passerine-like flight, which is spreading south from Hawke's Bay, colonising shingle rivers, to the South Island. Flocking in autumn, it nests on shingle and feeds at the water's edge.

WRYBILL *Anarhynchus frontalis* 20 cm A very approachable bird with a unique right-turning bill, the Wrybill runs fast with its head tucked in or rests or hops on one leg. It nests on large river beds in Canterbury and winters at Firth of Thames, Manukau and Kaipara.

SHORE PLOVER *Thinornis novaeseelandiae* 20 cm With wing patterns and coloration rather like a Turnstone, this bird is confined to Southeast Island in the Chathams. Pairs make co-ordinated zig-zag courtship flights. It feeds in salt or brackish pools and nests in petrel burrows or crevices or under roots.

TURNSTONE *Arenaria interpres* 23 cm Robust, with relatively short legs, Turnstones are holarctic breeders occurring in flocks throughout the country and on Auckland and Chatham Islands. They prefer rough shores with pools and flip over seaweed and stones with their bills.

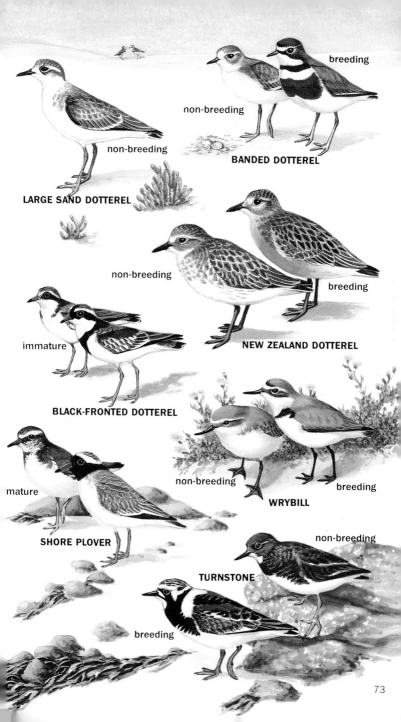

non-breeding

breeding

BANDED DOTTEREL

non-breeding

LARGE SAND DOTTEREL

non-breeding

breeding

NEW ZEALAND DOTTEREL

immature

BLACK-FRONTED DOTTEREL

non-breeding

breeding

WRYBILL

mature

SHORE PLOVER

non-breeding

TURNSTONE

breeding

73

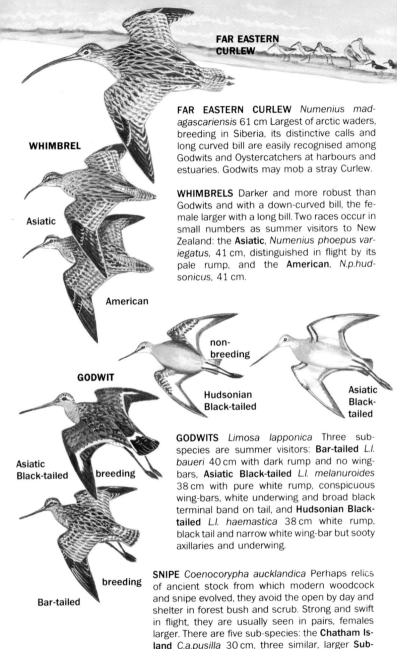

FAR EASTERN CURLEW *Numenius madagascariensis* 61 cm Largest of arctic waders, breeding in Siberia, its distinctive calls and long curved bill are easily recognised among Godwits and Oystercatchers at harbours and estuaries. Godwits may mob a stray Curlew.

WHIMBRELS Darker and more robust than Godwits and with a down-curved bill, the female larger with a long bill. Two races occur in small numbers as summer visitors to New Zealand: the **Asiatic**, *Numenius phoepus variegatus,* 41 cm, distinguished in flight by its pale rump, and the **American**, *N.p.hudsonicus,* 41 cm.

GODWITS *Limosa lapponica* Three subspecies are summer visitors: **Bar-tailed** *L.l. baueri* 40 cm with dark rump and no wing-bars, **Asiatic Black-tailed** *L.l. melanuroides* 38 cm with pure white rump, conspicuous wing-bars, white underwing and broad black terminal band on tail, and **Hudsonian Black-tailed** *L.l. haemastica* 38 cm white rump, black tail and narrow white wing-bar but sooty axillaries and underwing.

SNIPE *Coenocorypha aucklandica* Perhaps relics of ancient stock from which modern woodcock and snipe evolved, they avoid the open by day and shelter in forest bush and scrub. Strong and swift in flight, they are usually seen in pairs, females larger. There are five sub-species: the **Chatham Island** *C.a.pusilla* 30 cm, three similar, larger **Subantarctic** races and the **Stewart Island**, possibly now extinct.

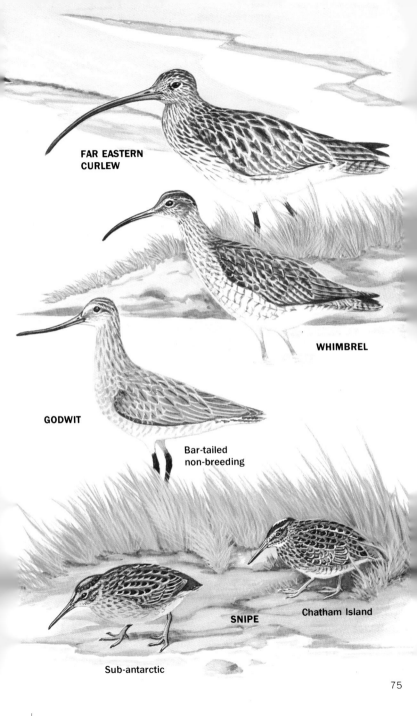

FAR EASTERN CURLEW

WHIMBREL

GODWIT

Bar-tailed
non-breeding

SNIPE

Chatham Island

Sub-antarctic

75

KNOT

KNOT *Calidris canutus* 25 cm Found in large flocks, with Godwits, on northern harbour tidelines, salt marshes and coastal flats, or in unmixed flocks on sandy beaches, they breed in Siberia. Some 'red' Knots overwinter in New Zealand.

PECTORAL SANDPIPER *Calidris melanotus* 22 cm Like the Sharp-tailed Sandpiper but lacking flank markings, and bill slightly down-curved, its carrying call note is 'kreek'.

SHARP-TAILED SANDPIPER *Calidris acuminata* 22 cm A regular and numerous migrant from Siberia, this sandpiper never looks grey. Its speckled browns make it conspicuous amongst Wrybills.

CURLEW SANDPIPER *Calidris ferruginea* 22 cm This Wrybill-sized bird has a distinctly down-curved bill. Its white upper-tail coverts and wing bar show in flight. It feeds among Knots at tidelines.

SANDERLING *Calidris alba* 20 cm An arctic breeder, usually alone and always running, this bird has small dark patches on the wing joints. Underparts, head and breast become pale chestnut in April.

RED-NECKED STINT *Calidris ruficollis* 15 cm Stints, usually grey, become red before they leave for the Arctic in April. Some first-year birds overwinter and associate with Wrybills.

TEREK SANDPIPER *Tringa cinerea* 23 cm Frequenting tidal flats, often with Wrybills, the Terek has an up-curved beak and bright yellow legs. In flight the white rear-edge of the wings is conspicuous.

WANDERING TATTLER *Tringa incana* 28 cm An Alaskan breeder, hard to distinguish from the **Siberian Tattler** *T.brevipes* except when in breeding plumage when underparts are heavily barred, the Siberian staying white.

Wandering
Tattler
breeding

Siberian
Tattler

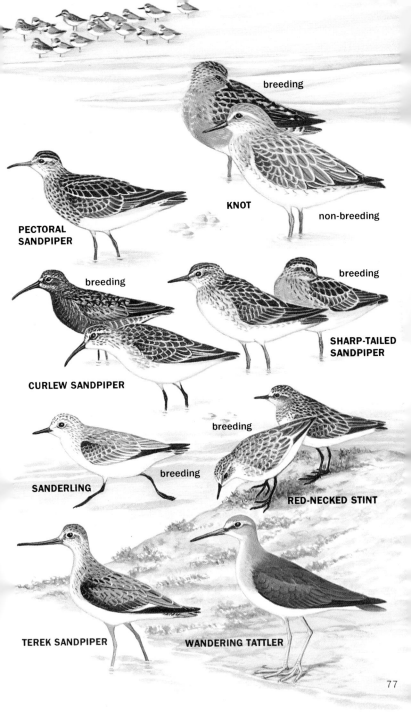

breeding

KNOT

non-breeding

**PECTORAL
SANDPIPER**

breeding

breeding

**SHARP-TAILED
SANDPIPER**

CURLEW SANDPIPER

breeding

SANDERLING

breeding

RED-NECKED STINT

TEREK SANDPIPER

WANDERING TATTLER

77

LEAST GOLDEN PLOVER *Pluvialis fulva* 25 cm
These shy birds form flocks and may venture short distances inland. They acquire breeding plumage before leaving for north-east Asia and western Alaska.

GREY PLOVER *Pluvialis squatarola* 28 cm
Generally seen alone in winter plumage, the Grey is larger and lighter-coloured than the Golden Plover. In flight black axillaries are visible. These plovers are cosmopolitan, circumpolar breeders.

non-breeding

ORIENTAL DOTTEREL *Charadrius veredus* 25 cm These rare summer visitors from north Asia, seen in small flocks or singly amongst other plovers on dry mud near lagoons (seldom near the sea) bob their heads when alarmed. They have longer legs and a more upright stance than the Golden Plover.

non-breeding

breeding

MONGOLIAN DOTTEREL *Charadrius mongolus* 19 cm In juvenile or non-breeding dress hard to tell from Banded Dotterel, this bird has a longer, deeper bill, an upright stance and the dark behind its eye continues to the bill in front. It may acquire breeding dress before leaving New Zealand.

non-breeding

breeding

LITTLE WHIMBREL *Numenius minutus* 33 cm Resembling the Golden Plover in shape and colour, this bird has longer looking wings, dark primaries and a strongly down-curved bill. When tides force it off the flats it may be found in grassy paddocks with other dotterels and plovers.

JAPANESE SNIPE *Gallinago hardwickii* 33 cm A typical snipe with a rapid, twisting flight after a whirring take-off when almost underfoot. It has a long bill, short legs, distinct streaks on its head and a chestnut band on its tail. It creeps through grassy swamps probing the mud as it feeds.

GREENSHANK *Tringa nebularia* 33 cm Slimmer and more elegant than the Little Whimbrel, the Greenshank looks black and white when flying and has a white lower back and rump. An occasional visitor from the northern hemisphere, it likes muddy creeks and lagoons and the company of Pied Stilts. It has been seen at most coastal waders' haunts.

MARSH SANDPIPER *Tringa stagnatalis* 25 cm Like a smaller Greenshank, but with proportionately longer legs, and stilt-like in flight, this rare visitor from the palaearctic prefers fresh or brackish pools. It is seen singly with Pied Stilts.

non-breeding

breeding

BROAD-BILLED SANDPIPER *Limicola falcinellus* 18 cm A small sandpiper, snipe-shaped with a distinctively streaked head and down-curved tip to its bill, this bird is a very rare visitor from the arctic which should be watched for in northern harbours amongst Wrybills.

RED-NECKED PHALAROPE *Phalaropus lobatus* 19 cm Breeding in the arctic, this bird winters in seas around Borneo and New Guinea. Sometimes, blown off-course, a rare visitor reaches New Zealand. Graceful little birds, they have semi-webbed feet and thick under-plumage which traps cushions of air on which they float. A circumpolar species, they have a swift and erratic flight and are often found in flocks. They will spin round in the water and feed on the insects they disturb. Females are larger and brighter than males.

ORIENTAL PRATINCOLE *Glareola maldivarum* 23 cm Pratincoles are unusual birds to watch. They run rapidly on 'tip-toe' or hawk insects in flight, showing the chestnut markings under their wings, and look like big brown swallows. Very rare visitors to New Zealand, they breed in Asia in deserts or the drier parts of marshes.

ANTARCTIC SKUA

SOUTHERN SKUA

ANTARCTIC SKUA *Stercorarius maccormicki* 53 cm Adult Antarctic Skuas have yellow feathers on their necks and conspicuous white patches on the wings. They catch fish and krill but also chase other species until they drop or disgorge their food, and eat eggs and young birds. They migrate north from antarctic nesting sites near penguin colonies and winter at sea as far as the northern hemisphere. They have loud display calls. They lay two eggs. Chicks are pale grey.

SOUTHERN SKUA *Stercorarius skua lonnbergi* 62 cm Like the Antarctic Skuas but larger and darker brown overall. The adults have white wing patches. Their habits are like those of the Antarctic. They breed on Chatham, Stewart and on most of the sub-antarctic islands of New Zealand. They lay two eggs. Their downy chicks are brown.

ARCTIC SKUA *Stercorarius parasiticus* 43 cm The most frequently seen skua, noticeable as it harries other species for food, the Arctic has dark and light forms with various intermediate mottled immature plumages. A summer visitor to New Zealand, it is often seen near breeding colonies of White-fronted Terns but seldom has its central tail feathers fully grown.

POMARINE SKUA *Stercorarius pomarinus* 48 cm The Pomarine Skua has more white on its wings than the Arctic. It too has dark and light forms, but, when fully grown, the twisted central tail feathers distinguish it. The immature has a paler rump. A summer visitor to New Zealand, it harries flocks of waders and gull and tern colonies.

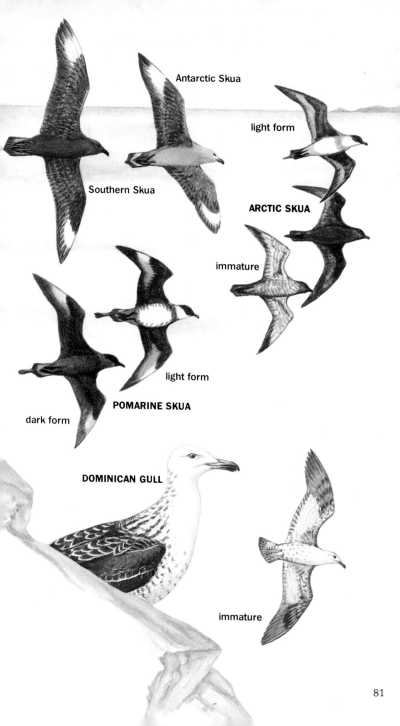

Antarctic Skua

light form

Southern Skua

ARCTIC SKUA

immature

light form

POMARINE SKUA

dark form

DOMINICAN GULL

immature

immature

breeding

non-breeding

DOMINICAN GULL *Larus dominicanus* 60 cm Immature birds, mottled brown in their first plumage, change in stages until adult dress is acquired in their third year. The immature plumage is not uniform and individuals vary. This sedentary species is common throughout coastal areas, often feeding inland and scavenging. It nests along coasts in colonies, laying three eggs. Chicks are blotchy grey. (Another illustration page 81.)

BLACK-BILLED GULL *Larus bulleri* 37 cm Less of a scavenger than the other two gulls, this bird eats live prey including insects. Largely an inland bird, it is common in the South Island. Immature birds have pink bills and legs. It nests in colonies, mainly on shingle river beds, and lake shores and sometimes on estuaries. It lays two eggs.

RED-BILLED GULL *Larus novaehollandiae scopulinus* 37 cm Scavenging more on man than the Black-billed, this gull breeds and nests around the coasts, sometimes forming mixed colonies with the Black-billed Gulls, as on Lake Rotorua. Immatures have dark bills and legs. Two to three eggs are laid.

CASPIAN TERN *Hydroprogne caspia* 51 cm The largest tern, its immatures like adults in non-breeding dress, the Caspian is common on the coasts of main islands and fishes the shallow waters of estuaries, rivers and inland lakes. A colonial nester on coasts although single pairs can be found breeding on lakes inland. One to three eggs are laid.

Immature
Ngoiro

DOMINICAN GULL

BLACK-BILLED GULL

immature

immature

RED-BILLED GULL

breeding **CASPIAN TERN**

83

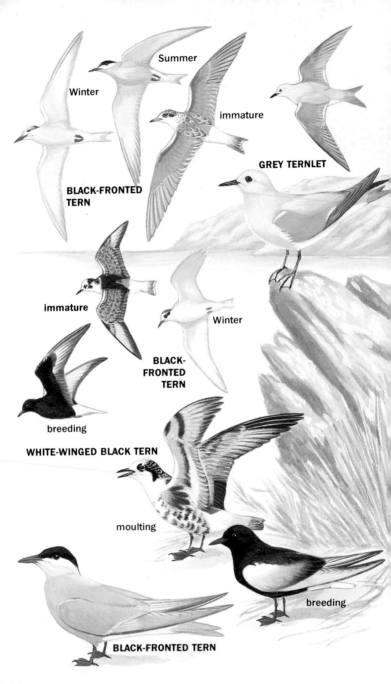

Winter

Summer

immature

BLACK-FRONTED TERN

GREY TERNLET

immature

Winter

BLACK-FRONTED TERN

breeding

WHITE-WINGED BLACK TERN

moulting

breeding

BLACK-FRONTED TERN

WHITE-CAPPED NODDY

immature

WHITE TERN

WHITE-CAPPED NODDY *Anous minutus* 34 cm Seldom seen round main islands unless blown there by gales, this bird nests in trees or rocks on Norfolk Island and the Kermadecs.

WHITE TERN *Gygis alba candida* 31 cm Swift and erratic fliers, terns' wings seem translucent against the light. They lay one egg, blunt at both ends, high on a tree branch on Norfolk Island and the Kermadecs.

GREY TERNLET *Procelsterna cerulea albivitta* 28 cm This long-legged bird screams noisily in flight and 'purrs' on its nesting cliffs on Lord Howe, Norfolk, Kermadec and Three Kings Islands where it nests in shady niches under vegetation or boulders.

WHITE-WINGED BLACK TERN *Chlidonias leucopterus* 23 cm Distinctive terns in black breeding dress, these birds have various puzzling plumages. They frequent marshes and shallow pools and have a swift and agile flight, hawking insects almost on the water surface or snapping them up as they walk on muddy ground.

BLACK-FRONTED TERN *Chlidonias hybrida albostriatus* 30 cm Smaller and greyer than the White-fronted, this bird has a white rump, noticeable in flight. The common inland tern in the South Island, it forms nesting colonies, often near Black-billed Gulls, and lays 1–3 eggs in a shingle scrape.

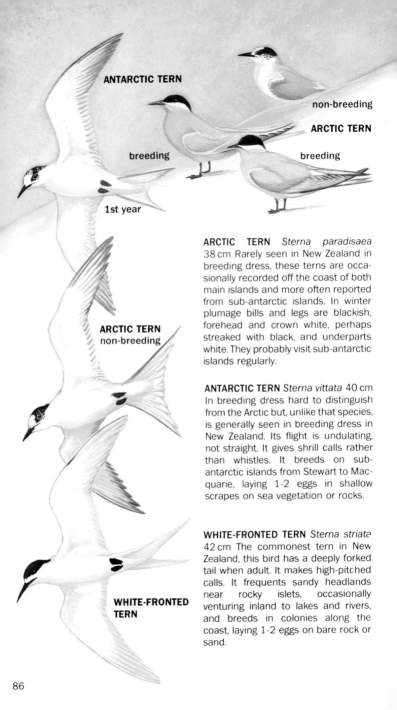

ANTARCTIC TERN

ARCTIC TERN
non-breeding

ARCTIC TERN
breeding

breeding

1st year

ARCTIC TERN
non-breeding

WHITE-FRONTED TERN

ARCTIC TERN *Sterna paradisaea* 38 cm Rarely seen in New Zealand in breeding dress, these terns are occasionally recorded off the coast of both main islands and more often reported from sub-antarctic islands. In winter plumage bills and legs are blackish, forehead and crown white, perhaps streaked with black, and underparts white. They probably visit sub-antarctic islands regularly.

ANTARCTIC TERN *Sterna vittata* 40 cm In breeding dress hard to distinguish from the Arctic but, unlike that species, is generally seen in breeding dress in New Zealand. Its flight is undulating, not straight. It gives shrill calls rather than whistles. It breeds on sub-antarctic islands from Stewart to Macquarie, laying 1-2 eggs in shallow scrapes on sea vegetation or rocks.

WHITE-FRONTED TERN *Sterna striata* 42 cm The commonest tern in New Zealand, this bird has a deeply forked tail when adult. It makes high-pitched calls. It frequents sandy headlands near rocky islets, occasionally venturing inland to lakes and rivers, and breeds in colonies along the coast, laying 1-2 eggs on bare rock or sand.

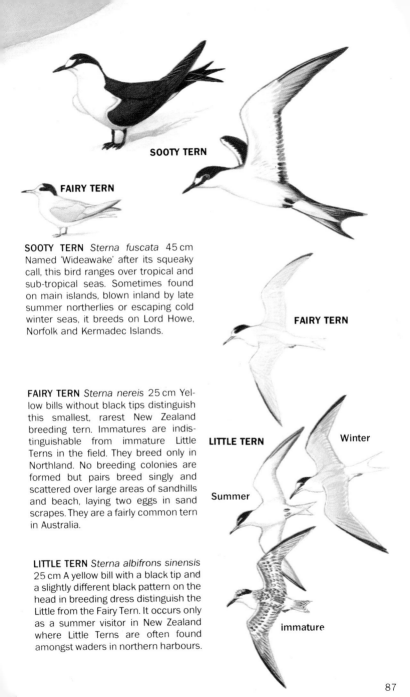

SOOTY TERN

FAIRY TERN

FAIRY TERN

LITTLE TERN

Winter

Summer

immature

SOOTY TERN *Sterna fuscata* 45 cm
Named 'Wideawake' after its squeaky
call, this bird ranges over tropical and
sub-tropical seas. Sometimes found
on main islands, blown inland by late
summer northerlies or escaping cold
winter seas, it breeds on Lord Howe,
Norfolk and Kermadec Islands.

FAIRY TERN *Sterna nereis* 25 cm Yellow bills without black tips distinguish
this smallest, rarest New Zealand
breeding tern. Immatures are indistinguishable from immature Little
Terns in the field. They breed only in
Northland. No breeding colonies are
formed but pairs breed singly and
scattered over large areas of sandhills
and beach, laying two eggs in sand
scrapes. They are a fairly common tern
in Australia.

LITTLE TERN *Sterna albifrons sinensis*
25 cm A yellow bill with a black tip and
a slightly different black pattern on the
head in breeding dress distinguish the
Little from the Fairy Tern. It occurs only
as a summer visitor in New Zealand
where Little Terns are often found
amongst waders in northern harbours.

**NEW ZEALAND
PIGEON**

NEW ZEALAND PIGEON *Hemiphaga novaeseelandiae* 51 cm The advent of the Europeans led to the decrease of this large bird but after protection it again became well-established in forest areas. It may be approached, cautiously, as it flaps about in trees, feeding on young leaves and fruit. It has a soft penetrating 'Ku', builds a flimsy twig nest in small branches 3-9 m from the ground and lays one white egg. It may have more than one brood.

ROCK PIGEON *Columba livia* 33 cm This is the well-known feral and city pigeon originating from escaped domestic strains and now gradually reverting to the plumage of its wild ancestor, the Rock Pigeon. Rock Pigeons make a variety of 'coos' and nest on buildings. Round West Auckland, Hawke's Bay and Bank's Peninsula they are feral, breeding naturally in caves of coastal and inland cliffs.

SPOTTED DOVE *Streptopelia chinensis tigriua* 30 cm This fast-flying bird has a spectacular display, flying upwards then gliding down with stiff wings and tail. Originally from Asia, it is feral around Auckland, frequenting well-wooded gardens and parks and feeding on the ground. All year round they coo with varying rhythm and emphasis. They build flimsy nests, hidden in tall trees, lay two white eggs and have more than one brood.

New Zealand Pigeon

Rock Pigeon

Spotted Dove

ROCK PIGEON

SPOTTED DOVE

KEA

KAKA

South Island

KAKAPO

90

KEA *Nestor notabilis* 46 cm Named for their calls, Keas live in the South Island mountains, feeding on roots, leaves, buds, fruit, nectar, insects and carrion. Some individuals will attack trapped and injured sheep. Males have longer upper mandibles which are less curved in the females. Very playful tame birds, they nest in hollows on the ground, laying 2–4 white eggs on twigs and leaves.

KAKA *Nestor meridionalis* 45 cm Named after their calls, Kakas are strong fliers which inhabit native forest on main and larger coastal islands. There are two subspecies. The **South Island** *N.m.meridionalis* is brighter-coloured than the **North Island** *N.m. septentrionalis*. Males' bills are more deeply curved. They dig in dying wood for grubs and eat fruit, leaves, nectar and insects. They nest in hollow trees and lay 4–5 white eggs on powdered wood.

WHITE COCKATOO *Cacatua galerita* 50 cm The colonies, established between the Lower Waikato and Raglan, between the watersheds of the Turakina and Rangitikei and near Wellington, grew from escapes or from birds released accidentally. Alert, gregarious, raucous, these strong fliers often feed on the ground and nest in tree hollows, laying 2–3 white eggs.

KAKAPO *Strigops habroptilus* 63 cm Males of this very, very rare 'Owl-parrot', as early colonists called it, are larger than females. Found near Milford Sound and on Stewart Island, their presence is indicated by forest tracks or loose balls of chewed tussock left on the plants. Nocturnal and flightless, although they can glide downwards for some distance. Males boom from dust bowls during the breeding season. They eat nectar, ferns, moss, lizards and fungi and lay 2–4 glossy-white eggs on powdered wood in holes and hollows.

North Island

WHITE COCKATOO

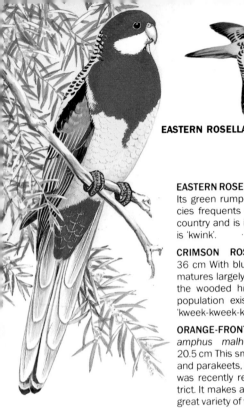

EASTERN ROSELLA

CRIMSON ROSELLA

EASTERN ROSELLA *Platycercus eximius* 33 cm Its green rump noticeable in flight, this species frequents orchards and lightly wooded country and is increasing in numbers. Its call is 'kwink'.

CRIMSON ROSELLA *Platycercus elegans* 36 cm With blue cheeks and throat and immatures largely green, this species frequents the wooded hills near Wellington. A hybrid population exists near Dunedin. Its call is 'kweek-kweek-kweek'.

ORANGE-FRONTED PARAKEET *Cyanoramphus malherbi* male 22 cm, female 20.5 cm This smallest and rarest of New Zealand parakeets, less yellow and a purer green, was recently recorded from the Nelson district. It makes a rapid chattering noise, eats a great variety of vegetation and nests in hollow trees, laying eggs on powdered wood.

YELLOW-CROWNED PARAKEET *Cyanoramphus auriceps* male 25.5 cm, female 23 cm Once widely distributed on both main islands but now fairly common only in large forest tracts the Yellow-crowned has no red behind the eye. It feeds on fewer ground plants than the Orange-fronted, has calls of higher pitch and similar nesting habits.

RED-CROWNED PARAKEET *Cyanoramphus novaezelandiae* male 28 cm, female 25.5 cm Because they damaged orchards the Red-crowned were persecuted and decreased. Now rare, they are confined to larger forest tracts on the main islands. Populations on smaller islands flourish. They have a rapid flight and fast chatter. Their nesting habits are like other parakeets.

ANTIPODES PARAKEET *Cyanoramphus unicolor* male 31.5 cm, female 29 cm Largest of the native parakeets, the Antipodes feeds on the remains from penguin colonies, eggs and carcasses. It has the softest voice. It nests on the ground, in holes or at the base of tall tussock. All native parakeets lay white eggs.

YELLOW-CROWNED
PARAKEET

ORANGE-FRONTED
PARAKEET

RED-CROWNED PARAKEET

ANTIPODES PARAKEET

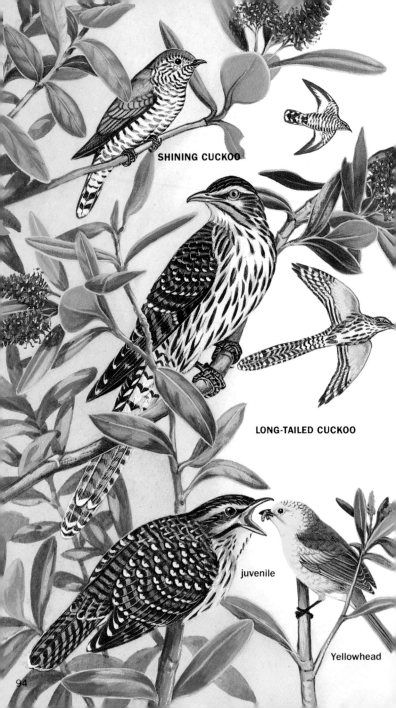

SHINING CUCKOO

LONG-TAILED CUCKOO

juvenile

Yellowhead

SHINING CUCKOO *Chalcites lucidus* 16 cm The female lacks the male's white eye-stripe, has purplish-tinged head feathers and breast bars that are more bronze. More often heard than seen, this small cuckoo needs a good light to show off its beautiful colours. Its musical whistle is heard day and night after its arrival in late September, particularly when several chase each other in and out of tall trees. It is found throughout main and Stewart Islands, feeding on insects and hairy caterpillars of the magpie moth. Singing stops when it leaves in February to winter in the Pacific. Generally its variable eggs are laid in the nests of Grey Warblers but it also parasitises Fantails, Tomtits, Silvereyes, Chatham Island Warblers and small introduced birds.

LONG-TAILED CUCKOO *Eudynamys taitensis* 40 cm The female is smaller and more rufous. This cuckoo has a strong glide-broken flight and looks not unlike a falcon in shape. Its unique harsh screeches, most often heard at night, may be the only sign of its October arrival. It parasitises Whiteheads and Yellowheads, laying its variable eggs in the nests of these and other species. Tuis dislike it and Bellbirds mob it. In early February Long-tailed Cuckoos form small flocks and migrate over large areas of the south-west Pacific.

BROAD-BILLED ROLLER

BROAD-BILLED ROLLER *Eurystomus orientalis pacificus* 29 cm Immatures are more dull in colour, lack red beaks and have greenish throats. These rollers are clumsy birds, usually seen alone or in pairs and unable to manoeuvre in dense forest. They perch conspicuously in tree tops waiting for large insects which they batter on branches. They migrate from the tropics, breeding in Australia. Young may drift to New Zealand in late summer. Their call is harsh and repetitive.

LITTLE OWL

LITTLE OWL *Athene noctua* 23 cm Whiter-faced and shorter-tailed than Moreporks, Little Owls have a dipping flight and are often seen hunting over open country by day. They will dig for earthworms in full sunlight and have a variety of soft and strident calls. Introduced from Europe, they are established throughout the South Island, except in mountain ranges. They nest in holes in trees or buildings and lay 2–3 white eggs.

MOREPORK *Ninox novaeseelandiae* 29 cm Named for its call, this bird is more nocturnal than the Little Owl and may be seen hunting at dusk. It hawks from a perch for large insects, taking some by talons in mid-air, spiders, small mammals, lizards and, on outliers, small petrels. Established in settled and forest areas throughout New Zealand (but not on Chatham or sub-antarctic isles) it makes its nest in hollow trees or clumps of vegetation (Astelia) and lays 2–3 white eggs.

MOREPORK

New Zealand Kingfisher

KOOKABURRA

KOOKABURRA *Dacelo novaeguineae* 45 cm A large quiet-coloured kingfisher which escapes notice by sitting motionless on poles or stumps. It gives loud, raucous laughs at dawn and dusk: one bird starts, others in the vicinity joining in. Established from introduced stock on Kawau Island it has now spread to the western shores of Hauraki Gulf between Auckland and Cape Rodney. They have been reported elsewhere and are thought originally to have been windblown from Australia. Nests are in holes in trees or banks and 2–4 white eggs are laid.

immature

NEW ZEALAND KINGFISHER *Halcyon sancta vagans* 24 cm Human settlement probably helped this kingfisher's spread and it has a wide range of habitats including open forest and coastal areas. Common in the North Island and most outliers, scarcer in the South Island, it is not found in Chatham or sub-antarctic islands. It dives at its prey: insects, fish and small animals of all kinds. The 10–23 cm upward-inclining nesting tunnel and chamber, made by the bird flying bill-first at banks or rotten trees, has no nesting material and 4–5 white eggs are laid. The nests may be used for many years.

NEW ZEALAND KINGFISHER

FORK-TAILED SWIFT

SPINE-TAILED SWIFT

WELCOME SWALL

AUSTRALIAN TREE MARTIN

98

SPINE-TAILED SWIFT *Chaetura caudacuta* 20 cm Swifts, the world's fastest flying birds, are insectivorous and glue their nests together with saliva. Unable to perch on their forward-facing toes, they feed, drink, preen, sleep – and may even mate – on the wing. Spine-tails breed in eastern Asia, migrate regularly as far as Tasmania and straggle to New Zealand. Some probably come each year, occasionally many. White throats and under-tail coverts are noticeable in flight, the protruding spines are not.

FORK-TAILED SWIFT *Apus pacificus* 18 cm In Australia this swift associates with the Spine-tailed, keeping up a constant twittering and chattering. They also mob, rather ineffectively, birds of prey. It is the smaller species, distinguished by tail shape and white rump. It breeds in east Asia, migrates south and stragglers may be seen off New Zealand coasts. They fly very high unless hawking insects or forced low over the water by bad weather.

AUSTRALIAN TREE MARTIN *Hylochelidon nigricans* 14 cm At first glance like the Welcome Swallow, but the tail is only slightly forked, this bird has a dull whitish rump, throat and breast and greyish under-tail coverts. It hawks insects over water, hovering and dipping and making twittering noises. It breeds in holes in trees and buildings in Australia and is an irregular visitor to New Zealand. Stragglers or small flocks are found especially around Nelson, Farewell Spit and in the far south.

WELCOME SWALLOW *Hirundo tahitica neoxena* 15 cm A rufous throat and chest and a deeply-forked tail, seen from below to be sub-terminally white, distinguish this bird from the Tree Martin. Immatures of both species are duller than adults. A rare visitor before 1958, it is now common throughout the main islands in all suitable habitats.

RIFLEMAN

♀

♂

BUSH WREN

♀

♂

ROCK WREN

♀

♂

immature

SILVEREYE

RIFLEMAN *Acanthisitta chloris* 8 cm Found south of the northern third of the North Island, in the South Island, Stewart, Great and Little Barrier Islands, this bird's high-pitched calls give its position away as it searches bark crevices for insects and spiders. Nests, in hollow branches or banks of old bush roads, are loosely woven and 4-5 white eggs laid. Males are often polygamous.

BUSH WREN *Xenicus longipes* 9.5 cm This wren feeds largely on insects in the foliage and bobs its whole body vigorously when alighting. It makes subdued trills, rasping notes and loud cheeps. Three subspecies are known: North Island, South Island and Stead's Bush Wren, all of which are now exceedingly rare, if not actually extinct.

ROCK WREN *Xenipes gilviventris* 9.5 cm Rock Wrens frequent open rock and talus slopes at altitudes of 750-2,500 m, mainly in the Southern Alps. Bobbing vigorously, they feed on insects, fruit, alpine plants and have a three-note call and thin pipe. A globular nest of moss and lichen, lined with feathers, is built in a crevice and 1-5 white eggs are laid. Both parents feed the young.

SILVEREYE *Zosterops lateralis* 12 cm Silvereyes came over from Australia in 1856 and are now common up to 1,000 m in all types of settled habitat with tree cover including native forest and sub-alpine scrub. Aggressive birds with varied calls, they flock in autumn and winter. Mainly insectivorous, they love nectar and are easily fed with fat, fruit and syrup. Their nests are cups of woven grass suspended from twigs 1-9 m above the ground. Both birds incubate the 3-4 pale blue eggs.

Black phase

FANTAIL

FANTAIL *Rhipidura fuliginosa* 16 cm Common in forest, tree and scrub-covered settled districts, Fantails are insectivorous, inquisitive and lively, posturing with spread tails. Two colour phases occur: Black (very rare on North Island) and Pied. They have penetrating notes. The small cobweb-covered nests of fibre and moss are built, 3-4 spotted cream eggs incubated and young fed by both birds. Five broods have been recorded in one season (August-January).

TOMTIT *Petroica macrocephala* 13 cm Largely sedentary, aggressive birds, Tomtit island subspecies include: **North Island** *P.m.toitoi*, **South Island** *P.m.macrocephala* and **Snares Island** (or **Black**) *P.m.dannefaerdi*. Their original range, reduced by forest clearance, is expanding under settled conditions. They dart from perches after insects on bark or ground. Calls and songs are varied. Pairs remain together, regularly examining intruders. Females build moss, bark and cobweb nests in tree or rock crevices, sometimes in tree forks, and incubate two broods of 3-5 spotted cream eggs. Both birds feed the young.

ROBIN *Petroica australis* 18 cm Sedentary, territorial, aggressive and inquisitive birds with three subspecies: **North Island** *P.a.longipes*, **South Island** *P.a.australis* and **Stewart Island** *P.a.rakiura* (very similar to *P.a.longipes*). Sexes differ slightly. Originally of forest and scrub they enter secondary growth and the exotic plantations on the Volcanic Plateau, feeding on invertebrates. Their varied song builds up until the bush rings. Bulky fibre nests, cobweb-bound and tree fern-lined, are sited low. Females incubate 2-3 spotted cream eggs. Males feed the young.

BLACK ROBIN *Petroica traversi* 16 cm A black species similar to the Robin, found only on Mangere Island.

SOUTH ISLAND
TOMTIT

♂

SNARES ISLAND
TOMTIT

NORTH ISLAND
TOMTIT

♂

NORTH ISLAND ROBIN

SOUTH ISLAND
ROBIN

BLACK
ROBIN

103

WHITEHEAD

YELLOWHEAD

BROWN CREEPER

GREY WARBLER

immature

CHATHAM ISLAND WARBLER
Gerygone albofrontata 12 cm Originally found throughout Chatham Islands in native forest, now only in remnants in the southern part of Chatham, Pitt, South-East and Little Mangere Islands. Habits, nest and eggs are like the Grey. Its call repeats three weak notes with breaks between.

CHATHAM ISLAND WARBLER

WHITEHEAD *Mohoua albicilla* 15 cm Found in native and exotic forests south of Northland, on Great and Little Barrier, Arid and Kapiti Islands. Whiteheads are noisy and inquisitive. Flocks actively search trunks and branches for insects, chirping like sparrows. They build cup-shaped nests in shrubs, tree canopies or forks.

YELLOWHEAD *Mohoua ochrocephala* 15 cm Found in large areas of native forest in the South Island, and possibly Stewart, Yellowheads make 6-8-note calls as they vigorously search for insects in the tops of trees. Cup-shaped nests are built high in cavities in dying wood. Young are first fed by regurgitation. Males are often polygamous.

BROWN CREEPER *Finschia novaeseelandiae* 13 cm Found in native forest but venturing into adjacent exotic vegetation, in South, Stewart and outlier islands. Flocks or pairs search bark and leaves for insects, nest in the canopy or in vines and make harsh repetitive calls. Females are fed by males while incubating the eggs.

GREY WARBLER *Gerygone igata* 11 cm These insectivorous warblers, dispersed from native forest and well-adapted to settler conditions, are found, usually in pairs, in all districts up to 1,400 m altitudes. They trill a sweet, varied song. Their pear-shaped nest, suspended 1.6-7.5 m above the ground, has a side entrance near the top.

FERNBIRD

FERNBIRD *Bowdleria punctata* 18 cm Widespread locally in drier swamps adjoining rough land, pairs of Fernbirds keep in contact with their double calls, a sharp metallic note and a soft click. Males give one, females answer with the other. Nests are deep in sedges, rushes or low vegetation. Six subspecies are recognized.

immature

♀

♂

immature

BLACKBIR

part albino

SONG THRUSH

immature

106

Skylark

BLACKBIRD *Turdus merula* 25 cm Introduced from Europe, Blackbirds are found through New Zealand up to altitudes of 1,400 m and have colonised offshore islands and outliers from the Kermadecs to Campbell Island. Part albinos are common. They have most beautiful songs and strident alarm calls. They like fruit, though feed mostly on the ground on invertebrates. Their nests, strengthened with mud, are generally low in bushes, often in outbuildings. They lay 2-5 greenish-blue eggs freckled with red-brown.

SONG THRUSH *Turdus philomelos* 23 cm A European introduction, Song Thrushes are found in all types of country, even dense bush, up to altitudes of 1,300 m, and on outlying islands from the Kermadecs to Campbell Island. They feed on insects, berries, and fruit and crack snail shells on 'anvil' stones. They have a loud, clear musical song and occasionally mimic other birds. They lay 3-6 blueish-green, black-speckled eggs in a conspicuous, mud-lined nest, seldom far above ground and often in outbuildings.

NEW ZEALAND PIPIT *Anthus novaeseelandiae* 19 cm Common and wide-spread on rougher farmland, river beds and open country, but not in grass pastures, Pipits have varied, high-pitched calls. Stragglers reach offshore islands. They mostly feed on insects, taking some on the wing, but will eat some seeds. They nest at the base of tussock and lay 3-4 eggs.

SKYLARK *Alauda arvensis* 18 cm Skylarks have short crests and long hind claws and are common in open country and pastures up to altitudes of 1,600 m. Usually seen soaring overhead, delivering torrents of trills, they also sing on the ground. With strong undulating flight they sometimes 'shoot' with closed wings. A grass-lined ground hollow forms the nest for 3-7 speckled white eggs.

NEW ZEALAND PIPIT

SKYLARK

immature

TUI

BELLBIRD

♂

♀

TUI *Prosthemadera novaeseelandiae* male 31 cm, female 29 cm The Tui's song varies with the district and is interspersed with harsh noises. Noisy fliers through trees, they are sometimes acrobatic and dive with closed wings. Primarily a forest species, their range spreading into settled areas, they feed on insects, nectar and many fruits. Fine, grass-lined nests are built in outer forks or tree canopies on twig platforms. The female incubates the 2-4 eggs and feeds the chicks initially. The male helps later. Tui probably double brood.

BELLBIRD *Anthornis melanura* male 20 cm, female 19 cm A still-spreading forest species, Bellbirds are found throughout New Zealand, apart from around and north of Auckland. They feed on insects and fruit, hang upside down after nectar and bathe frequently. Their song of liquid, bell-like notes varies with the district. They make a deep, well-lined cup nest on a loose twig base well hidden in bush. They lay 3-4 eggs and both parents feed the chicks. They double breed.

STITCHBIRD *Notiomystis cincta* male 19 cm, female 18 cm Extinct on the mainland, Stitchbirds thrive on Little Barrier Island. More dependant upon nectar than the other two honey-eaters, they also eat insects and fruit. Both sexes make calls resembling 'stitch'. They live in various types of forest at all altitudes and lay 3-5 eggs in substantial nests lined with tree-fern scales and feathers, which they build on twig bases in holes in trees 3-18 m above ground.

STITCHBIRD

♂

♀

HOUSE SPARROW

♂

♀

♀ House Sparrow   Chaffinch ♀

HOUSE SPARROW *Passer domesticus* 14.5 cm Shipped to New Zealand and liberated in 1860, House Sparrows spread widely, colonising Chatham and other sub-antarctic islands. Partial albinos are not uncommon. They make a variety of chirps and nest in tall trees or buildings, laying 5-7 eggs.

YELLOWHAMMER *Emberiza citrinella* 16 cm Introduced and now ranging from sea beaches to alpine tussock at 1,600 m, Yellowhammers form flocks and visit gardens in autumn. In flight distinguished from the Cirl Bunting by its shining rusty rump. Stragglers cover considerable distances to offshore islands, breeding in Chatham and Raoul. They lay 3-5 eggs in a nest close to the ground.

CIRL BUNTING *Emberiza cirlus* 16 cm Also introduced, these rare birds resemble Yellowhammers but adult males have black throats. Found in limestone country near Oamaru, east of Southern Alps and recently in the North Island, they are nomadic in winter. Low-nesting, they lay 3-5 eggs.

HEDGE SPARROW *Prunella modularis* 14.5 cm Introduced to New Zealand, Hedge Sparrows have spread through the country as far as Campbell Island. They live in cover, from the coast up to altitudes of 1,600 m. Ground feeders, they fly seldom and have high-pitched calls. They nest low in thick vegetation and lay 3-5 eggs.

YELLOWHAMMER

♂

♀

♀

CIRL BUNTING

♀ Yellowhammer

♂

Cirl Bunting

♀

HEDGE SPARROW

111

GREENFINCH

GREENFINCH *Carduelis chloris* 15 cm
One of six introduced finches, widely if
unevenly distributed up to altitudes of
600 m, Greenfinches have colonised
the Chathams but are rarely found in
other offshore islands. They have a
pleasant twittering song and harsh
drawn-out calls. Forming flocks in autumn they often roost with House
Sparrows in winter in hedges and
shrubs. They nest up to 6 m above the
ground and lay 4-6 eggs.

GOLDFINCH *Carduelis carduelis* 12 cm
Sociable birds which live in large flocks
or family parties, Goldfinches are often
seen feeding on thistle heads and are
common over large areas of the main
islands but scarce above 1,000 m altitude. Large flocks frequent coastal
saltings in winter. They have liquid,
slightly metallic songs. They build
beautiful nests in leaves up to 3 m
above the ground and lay 4-6 eggs.

GOLDFINCH

REDPOLL

REDPOLL *Carduelis flammea* 12 cm The smallest introduced finch, with metallic flight calls, the Redpoll is often heard before it is seen. They are common throughout New Zealand, including offshore and sub-antarctic islands. After breeding they form flocks with other finches and favour coastal wasteland for winter feeding. They build small compact nests in shrubs, up to 3 m above ground, and lay 4-6 eggs.

CHAFFINCH *Fringilla coelebs* 15 cm The most common introduced species, sometimes more easily heard than seen, the Chaffinch is found wherever there are trees and shrubs up to altitudes of 1,400 m. They penetrate the bush as no other finch and are vigorous colonisers of offshore and sub-antarctic islands, breeding as far south as Campbell. Their metallic calls may form the dominant noise in northern beech forest above 1,000 m. They build beautiful nests of grass, roots, moss and lichens, placed in forks of trees. They lay 4-6 eggs.

CHAFFINCH

SOUTH ISLAND KOKAKO

KOKAKO *Callaeas cinerea* 38 cm There are two subspecies. In the **North Island** *C.c.wilsoni* is widely distributed, in the **South Island** *C.c.cinerea* survives, if at all, only in a few isolated areas. Both feed on flowers, fruit, leaves and probably on insects, hopping up and along trunks and branches and gliding from one tree top to another. They lay 2–3 eggs in finely-lined grass cups on wood fragments and twigs in a fork 2.5 m above the ground.

North Island race

NEW ZEALAND THRUSH

South Island race

immature

NORTH ISLAND KOKAKO

immature

NEW ZEALAND THRUSH *Turnagra capensis* 26 cm Both subspecies, **North Island** *T.c.tanagra* and **South Island** *T.c.capensis,* are possibly now extinct; although sightings in remote areas are still reported, none have been confirmed. An omnivorous forest floor feeder with a short rapid flight, this thrush builds a compact nest of twigs and moss 2 m above the ground and lays two eggs.

SADDLEBACK *Philesturnus carunculatus* 26 cm The **South Island** race *P. c. carunculatus* survived only on Cape Islands. Its immature, which has very different plumage, was once thought to be a separate species and called the Jackbird. The **North Island** *P.c.rufusater,* with juvenile like the adult, survived only on Hen Island. Both races have now been transferred elsewhere. Saddlebacks are omnivorous, territorial, pair throughout the year and have a clamorous song. They nest in dense cover near the ground in hollow trees and lay two eggs.

juvenile
Jackbird

SOUTH ISLAND SADDLEBACK

NORTH ISLAND SADDLEBACK

115

ROOK

ROOK *Corvus frugilegus* 45 cm Rooks were liberated several times in New Zealand and are now widely and unevenly distributed in both main islands, generally where crops are grown. If persecuted they disappear from an area and reappear in previously unrecorded districts. They feed on the ground on worms, insects, larvae and cultivated grain, roost communally and establish rookeries in tall exotic trees, such as pines, tall eucalyptus and Lombardy poplars. Rookeries are noisy and sociable places with much stealing of twigs from the neighbour's nest. Rooks hop and walk sedately, carry food in the bare white pouches under the bills, which juveniles lack (they have feathered faces), circle lazily in the air and make a variety of caws. They lay 2-5 eggs.

AUSTRALIAN MAGPIES *Gymnorhina tibicen* Magpies or Piping Crows were introduced from Australia late in the nineteenth century. They are not crows and do not 'pipe' but have wonderfully musical calls. The **White-backed Magpie** *G.t.hypoleuca* 42 cm is widely and unevenly distributed through both islands up to an altitude of 1,000 m and is still spreading. It generally nests in tall trees and, around Canterbury, in gorse and haw-thorn hedges. It sometimes lives side by side with the **Black-backed Magpie** *G.t.tibicen* 40 cm which has spread from North Canterbury to Marlborough and is well established in Hawke's Bay. Both favour grass-land with adjoining belts of trees where they dig for grubs and beetles.

BLACK-BACKED MAGPIE

♂

♀

immature

WHITE-BACKED MAGPIE

♂

♀

117

Winter

Summer

STARLING

immature

INDIAN MYNA

STARLING *Sturnus vulgaris* 21 cm Introduced in 1862, the European Starling is now abundant everywhere except in dense bush or at altitudes higher than 1,200 m and has spread to sub-antarctic islands. Highly pugnacious and adaptable, it controls and marshalls its young when danger threatens. It feeds, with busy rolling gait, on worms in ploughed fields, fruit from gardens or insects disturbed by the feet of grazing sheep and cattle. Noisy and gregarious, Starlings are clever mimics of other species, their own song acquires a 'local dialect' and may incorporate many artificial noises. Flocks mob enemies and make spectacular evening flights before settling into communal roosts. Opportunists, they make use of any hole in any place to nest, may introduce flowers into their nesting cavities and lay 4–7 pale blue eggs.

INDIAN MYNA *Acridotheres tristis* 24 cm The common Myna of southern India, introduced about a century ago, is now very common throughout the northern half of the North Island—north of Wanganui and southern Hawke's Bay. Large flocks frequent rubbish dumps, smaller numbers feed on the foreshore or ride the back of sheep and cattle picking off ticks and foraging for insects around their feet. They have a large range of squeaks, squawks or musical notes and the male makes ludicrous noises in breeding season. They form communal roosts in some localities, nest in holes in buildings, banks or trees and often include brightly-coloured flowers in nesting material. They lay 3–6 roundish blue eggs.

Index of common English names and Maori names

Note: A Maori name is sometimes used for more than one species or subspecies.

Index of Scientific Names